I0350330

==::== ॐ बाघेश्वराय नमः ॐ ==::==

—:: जय हनुमान -:ॐ:- जय सीताराम ::—

ONE CONSCIOUSNESS

FIERY WISDOM OF EKAM-SANĀTANA-DHARMA : BOOK EKAM

Belongs to ______________________

____

____

____

____

॥ एकं-सनातन-धर्म जयः ॥ - सीता राम - ॥ यतो धर्मस्ततो जयः ॥

ekaṁ sanātana-dharma jayaḥ :ॐ: yato dharmastato jayaḥ

Victory unto Ekam-Sanātana-Dharma - हनुमान - Where Dharma abides Victory abides.

Published by: only **RAMA** only
(an Imprint of e1i1 Corporation)

Title: ONE CONSCIOUSNESS
Sub-Title: FIERY WISDOM OF EKAM-SANĀTANA-DHARMA : BOOK EKAM

Author: Vijay Sanātani

Identifiers
ISBN: 978-1-945739-**59-0** (Paperback)
ISBN: 978-1-945739-**71-2** (Hardcover)

—o—

।। एकं-सनातन-धर्म जयः ।। ::—— जय हनुमान -:ॐ:- जय सीताराम ——:: ।। यतो धर्मस्ततो जयः ।।

DISCLAIMER

This Book is for entertainment purposes only and is purely fictional in nature.
Names, religions, characters, places, events, incidents, histories, years, statistics, percentages, numbers etc., mentioned are either the products of the author's imagination or used in a fictitious manner; and any resemblance to actuals is completely coincidental. All religions, nations, races, people, books, histories, places, events, timelines, statistic, data, numbers etc., referred to in this book—even those that might be construed by someone to have any resemblance to the existing ones of the present times—are entirely fictional and intended to be used in a fictitious manner, and categorically do not refer to any existing ones of the present age at all.
[- Please Also Read The Full Disclaimer A Few Pages Later -]

—o—

— ॐ —

CONTENTS

In this book, the prefix **BG, RCM, AG, YS, VCM** etc., in the Sanskrit verses represent:
bhagavad-gītā (BG); **rāmacharitamānas** (RCM); **aṣṭāvakra-gītā** (AG);
pātañjala-yoga-sūtra (YS); **vivek-chudāmani** (VCM).

Verses have been taken from: Tulsi Ramayana, Rāmcharitmānas with English Translation by Saxena et al. (ISBNs: 978-1-945739-**60-6**, 978-1-945739-**61-3**); Bhagavad Gītā by Sushma et al. (ISBNs: 978-1-945739-**36-1**, 978-1-945739-**37-8**); Vivekachudamani by Vidya Wati (ISBNs: 978-1-945739-**44-6**, 978-1-945739-**45-3**); Ashtavakra Gītā by Vidya Wati (ISBNs: 978-1-945739-**46-0**, 978-1-945739-**47-7**)

*Books in this **Fiery Wisdom of Ekam-Sanātana-Dharma** series:*

One Consciousness: Fiery Wisdom of Ekam-Sanātana-Dharma, Book **Ekam** (isbn:978-1-945739-**59-0**)
Non-Duality: Fiery Wisdom of Ekam-Sanātana-Dharma, Book **Dvit** (isbn:978-1-945739-**62-0**)
Beyond the Trinity: Fiery Wisdom of Ekam-Sanātana-Dharma, Book **Trit** (isbn:978-1-945739-**63-7**)
Turiya, the Fourth: Fiery Wisdom of Ekam-Sanātana-Dharma, Book **Chatur** (isbn:978-1-945739-**64-4**)
Beyond the Five: Fiery Wisdom of Ekam-Sanātana-Dharma, Book **Pancham** (isbn:978-1-945739-**65-1**)

Above books are all stand-alone and can be read independently, not necessarily sequentially. All books are ready but will be released only if the previous book in the series has sold at least a 100 copies—which could be quite a while considering that the followers of Sanātana-Dharma are few and far between. We have no reach or resources of our own and depend on just word-of-mouth recommendation; so if you do like this book, please consider telling other like-minded individuals. Thank you. Jai Sītā-Rāma-Hanumān

—ॐ—

श्रीसीतारामच्चरणार्पणमस्तु

śrī sītā-rāma caraṇā-arpaṇam-astu

सीताराम सीताराम सीताराम सीताराम सीताराम सीताराम सीताराम सीताराम सीताराम सीताराम सीताराम सीताराम सीताराम सीताराम सीताराम सीताराम सीताराम सीताराम

This book and its entire endeavor and fruits

Dedicated to
Lord-God Shri Sitā-Rāma

कायेन वाचा मनसेंद्रियैर्वा । बुद्ध्यात्मना वा प्रकृतिस्वभावात् ।
kāyena vācā manaseṁdriyairvā , buddhyātmanā vā prakṛtisvabhāvāt ,
करोमि यद्यत् सकलं परस्मै । नारायणायेति समर्पयामि ॥
karomi yadyat sakalaṁ parasmai , nārāyaṇāyeti samarpayāmi .

Whatever it is I do—through body, mind, speech, or sense-organs, or with my intellect and soul, or with my innate natural tendencies—whatever it be—I offer it all unto Nārāyana (Sitā-Rāma).

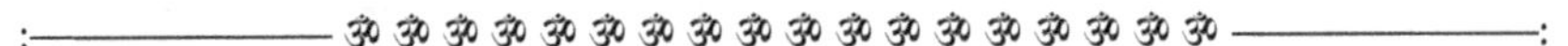

According to Sanātana-Dharma, there abides just one existence—Braham, the infinite ocean of consciousness which has become evolved into all this visible that we discern all around, and further the "I", or "Self" that is within us, abides rooted in that Divine-Being. Verily we are Divinity Himself—an ocean of bliss, immortal existence which never dies, which can never be hurt or killed. Sanātana-Dharma avers that our primary goal in life should be liberation—realizing who we are, realizing our oneness in Braham, the ocean of bliss; and the Sanātana-Dharma methods which teaches us that are called Yogas, meaning union—to become yoked to the Supreme. We can realize our true nature following any of the paths of Sanātana-Dharma: **Karma-Yoga, Bhakti-Yoga, Jnāna-Yoga, Rāja-Yoga**. There are seemingly endless scriptures in Sanātana-Dharma which lay out these various paths, and sometimes we end up getting confused with too many choices, but there are four scriptures which between themselves over-abundantly cover everything that needs to be known of Sanātana-Dharma: **bhagavad-gītā, rāmāyana, aṣṭāvakra-gītā, pātañjala-yoga-sūtra** which may also be said to reflect these four Yogas respectively. In fact bhagavad-gītā and rāmāyana both are perfect and complete in themselves needing nothing else, and we should always be reading a few verses from these two scriptures on a daily basis so that we always persist rooted in Sanātana-Dharma and never go astray. To be reminded of this, we have reproduced these scriptures in tiny fonts in the front and back of this book. Here please note that the valmiki-rāmāyana is in Sanskrit and its Avadhi rendering—the rāmacharitamānas of tulsidāsa—is not just in an easier language but is replete with Bhakti, and therefore very popular; and so we have used the **sundar-kānda** of **rāmacharitamānas** and printed that as the proxy for rāmāyana. The four Yogic paths reflect the diverse nature of men, and you will find at least one of paths resonating with your own inner nature, and thus following any or all of the paths laid out in these scriptures, you can make rapid spiritual progress and in finding your oneness in Braham and attain to emancipation. Finally if you find in any of my books something that contradicts the spirit, wisdom, essence of bhagavad-gītā and rāmāyana then simply reject it—it is probably the result of miscommunication at my end; my fault; thank you for your kindness. **Jai Hanumān, Jai Shri Sītā-Rāma.** [—AUTHOR]

bhagavad-gītā

ॐ

श्रीमद्भगवद्गीता

प्रथमोऽध्यायः - अर्जुनविषादयोगः

धृतराष्ट्र उवाच –

धर्मक्षेत्रे कुरुक्षेत्रे समवेता युयुत्सवः ।
मामकाः पाण्डवाश्चैव किमकुर्वत सञ्जय ॥१-१॥

सञ्जय उवाच –

दृष्ट्वा तु पाण्डवानीकं व्यूढं दुर्योधनस्तदा ।
आचार्यमुपसङ्गम्य राजा वचनमब्रवीत् ॥१-२॥
पश्यैतां पाण्डुपुत्राणामाचार्य महतीं चमूम् ।
व्यूढां द्रुपदपुत्रेण तव शिष्येण धीमता ॥१-३॥
अत्र शूरा महेष्वासा भीमार्जुनसमा युधि ।
युयुधानो विराटश्च द्रुपदश्च महारथः ॥१-४॥
धृष्टकेतुश्चेकितानः काशिराजश्च वीर्यवान् ।
पुरुजित्कुन्तिभोजश्च शैब्यश्च नरपुङ्गवः ॥१-५॥
युधामन्युश्च विक्रान्त उत्तमौजाश्च वीर्यवान् ।
सौभद्रो द्रौपदेयाश्च सर्व एव महारथाः ॥१-६॥
अस्माकं तु विशिष्टा ये तान्निबोध द्विजोत्तम ।
नायका मम सैन्यस्य संज्ञार्थं तान्ब्रवीमि ते ॥१-७॥
भवान्भीष्मश्च कर्णश्च कृपश्च समितिञ्जयः ।
अश्वत्थामा विकर्णश्च सौमदत्तिस्तथैव च ॥१-८॥
अन्ये च बहवः शूरा मदर्थे त्यक्तजीविताः ।

[illegible]

द्वितीयोऽध्यायः - साङ्ख्ययोगः

[illegible]

तृतीयोऽध्यायः - कर्मयोगः

[illegible]

चतुर्थोऽध्यायः - ज्ञानकर्मसंन्यासयोगः

[illegible]

पञ्चमोऽध्यायः - संन्यासयोगः

[illegible]

षष्ठोऽध्यायः - ध्यानयोगः

[illegible]

सप्तमोऽध्यायः - ज्ञानविज्ञानयोगः

[illegible]

अष्टमोऽध्यायः - अक्षरब्रह्मयोगः

[illegible]

नवमोऽध्यायः - राजविद्याराजगुह्ययोगः

[illegible]

त्रैविद्या मां सोमपाः पूतपापा यज्ञैरिष्ट्वा स्वर्गतिं प्रार्थयन्ते ।
ते पुण्यमासाद्य सुरेन्द्रलोकमश्नन्ति दिव्यान्दिवि देवभोगान् ॥ ९-२० ॥
ते तं भुक्त्वा स्वर्गलोकं विशालं क्षीणे पुण्ये मर्त्यलोकं विशन्ति ।
एवं त्रयीधर्ममनुप्रपन्ना गतागतं कामकामा लभन्ते ॥ ९-२१ ॥
अनन्याश्चिन्तयन्तो मां ये जनाः पर्युपासते ।
तेषां नित्याभियुक्तानां योगक्षेमं वहाम्यहम् ॥ ९-२२ ॥
येऽप्यन्यदेवता भक्ता यजन्ते श्रद्धयान्विताः ।
तेऽपि मामेव कौन्तेय यजन्त्यविधिपूर्वकम् ॥ ९-२३ ॥
अहं हि सर्वयज्ञानां भोक्ता च प्रभुरेव च ।
न तु मामभिजानन्ति तत्त्वेनातश्च्यवन्ति ते ॥ ९-२४ ॥
यान्ति देवव्रता देवान्पितॄन्यान्ति पितृव्रताः ।
भूतानि यान्ति भूतेज्या यान्ति मद्याजिनोऽपि माम् ॥ ९-२५ ॥
पत्रं पुष्पं फलं तोयं यो मे भक्त्या प्रयच्छति ।
तदहं भक्त्युपहृतमश्नामि प्रयतात्मनः ॥ ९-२६ ॥
यत्करोषि यदश्नासि यज्जुहोषि ददासि यत् ।
यत्तपस्यसि कौन्तेय तत्कुरुष्व मदर्पणम् ॥ ९-२७ ॥
शुभाशुभफलैरेवं मोक्ष्यसे कर्मबन्धनैः ।
संन्यासयोगयुक्तात्मा विमुक्तो मामुपैष्यसि ॥ ९-२८ ॥
समोऽहं सर्वभूतेषु न मे द्वेष्योऽस्ति न प्रियः ।
ये भजन्ति तु मां भक्त्या मयि ते तेषु चाप्यहम् ॥ ९-२९ ॥
अपि चेत्सुदुराचारो भजते मामनन्यभाक् ।
साधुरेव स मन्तव्यः सम्यग्व्यवसितो हि सः ॥ ९-३० ॥
क्षिप्रं भवति धर्मात्मा शश्वच्छान्तिं निगच्छति ।
कौन्तेय प्रतिजानीहि न मे भक्तः प्रणश्यति ॥ ९-३१ ॥
मां हि पार्थ व्यपाश्रित्य येऽपि स्युः पापयोनयः ।
स्त्रियो वैश्यास्तथा शूद्रास्तेऽपि यान्ति परां गतिम् ॥ ९-३२ ॥
किं पुनर्ब्राह्मणाः पुण्या भक्ता राजर्षयस्तथा ।
अनित्यमसुखं लोकमिमं प्राप्य भजस्व माम् ॥ ९-३३ ॥
मन्मना भव मद्भक्तो मद्याजी मां नमस्कुरु ।
मामेवैष्यसि युक्त्वैवमात्मानं मत्परायणः ॥ ९-३४ ॥

ॐ तत्सदिति श्रीमद्भगवद्गीतासूपनिषत्सु
ब्रह्मविद्यायां योगशास्त्रे श्रीकृष्णार्जुनसंवादे
राजविद्याराजगुह्ययोगो नाम नवमोऽध्यायः ॥

दशमोऽध्यायः - विभूतियोगः

श्रीभगवानुवाच –

भूय एव महाबाहो शृणु मे परमं वचः ।
यत्तेऽहं प्रीयमाणाय वक्ष्यामि हितकाम्यया ॥ १०-१ ॥
न मे विदुः सुरगणाः प्रभवं न महर्षयः ।
अहमादिर्हि देवानां महर्षीणां च सर्वशः ॥ १०-२ ॥
यो मामजमनादिं च वेत्ति लोकमहेश्वरम् ।
असम्मूढः स मर्त्येषु सर्वपापैः प्रमुच्यते ॥ १०-३ ॥
बुद्धिर्ज्ञानमसम्मोहः क्षमा सत्यं दमः शमः ।
सुखं दुःखं भवोऽभावो भयं चाभयमेव च ॥ १०-४ ॥
अहिंसा समता तुष्टिस्तपो दानं यशोऽयशः ।
भवन्ति भावा भूतानां मत्त एव पृथग्विधाः ॥ १०-५ ॥
महर्षयः सप्त पूर्वे चत्वारो मनवस्तथा ।
मद्भावा मानसा जाता येषां लोक इमाः प्रजाः ॥ १०-६ ॥
एतां विभूतिं योगं च मम यो वेत्ति तत्त्वतः ।
सोऽविकम्पेन योगेन युज्यते नात्र संशयः ॥ १०-७ ॥
अहं सर्वस्य प्रभवो मत्तः सर्वं प्रवर्तते ।
इति मत्वा भजन्ते मां बुधा भावसमन्विताः ॥ १०-८ ॥
मच्चित्ता मद्गतप्राणा बोधयन्तः परस्परम् ।
कथयन्तश्च मां नित्यं तुष्यन्ति च रमन्ति च ॥ १०-९ ॥
तेषां सततयुक्तानां भजतां प्रीतिपूर्वकम् ।
ददामि बुद्धियोगं तं येन मामुपयान्ति ते ॥ १०-१० ॥
तेषामेवानुकम्पार्थमहमज्ञानजं तमः ।
नाशयाम्यात्मभावस्थो ज्ञानदीपेन भास्वता ॥ १०-११ ॥

अर्जुन उवाच –

परं ब्रह्म परं धाम पवित्रं परमं भवान् ।
पुरुषं शाश्वतं दिव्यमादिदेवमजं विभुम् ॥ १०-१२ ॥
आहुस्त्वामृषयः सर्वे देवर्षिर्नारदस्तथा ।
असितो देवलो व्यासः स्वयं चैव ब्रवीषि मे ॥ १०-१३ ॥
सर्वमेतदृतं मन्ये यन्मां वदसि केशव ।
न हि ते भगवन्व्यक्तिं विदुर्देवा न दानवाः ॥ १०-१४ ॥
स्वयमेवात्मनात्मानं वेत्थ त्वं पुरुषोत्तम ।
भूतभावन भूतेश देवदेव जगत्पते ॥ १०-१५ ॥
वक्तुमर्हस्यशेषेण दिव्या ह्यात्मविभूतयः ।
याभिर्विभूतिभिर्लोकानिमांस्त्वं व्याप्य तिष्ठसि ॥ १०-१६ ॥
कथं विद्यामहं योगिंस्त्वां सदा परिचिन्तयन् ।
केषु केषु च भावेषु चिन्त्योऽसि भगवन्मया ॥ १०-१७ ॥
विस्तरेणात्मनो योगं विभूतिं च जनार्दन ।
भूयः कथय तृप्तिर्हि शृण्वतो नास्ति मेऽमृतम् ॥ १०-१८ ॥

श्रीभगवानुवाच –

हन्त ते कथयिष्यामि दिव्या ह्यात्मविभूतयः ।
प्राधान्यतः कुरुश्रेष्ठ नास्त्यन्तो विस्तरस्य मे ॥ १०-१९ ॥
अहमात्मा गुडाकेश सर्वभूताशयस्थितः ।
अहमादिश्च मध्यं च भूतानामन्त एव च ॥ १०-२० ॥
आदित्यानामहं विष्णुर्ज्योतिषां रविरंशुमान् ।
मरीचिर्मरुतामस्मि नक्षत्राणामहं शशी ॥ १०-२१ ॥
वेदानां सामवेदोऽस्मि देवानामस्मि वासवः ।
इन्द्रियाणां मनश्चास्मि भूतानामस्मि चेतना ॥ १०-२२ ॥
रुद्राणां शङ्करश्चास्मि वित्तेशो यक्षरक्षसाम् ।
वसूनां पावकश्चास्मि मेरुः शिखरिणामहम् ॥ १०-२३ ॥
पुरोधसां च मुख्यं मां विद्धि पार्थ बृहस्पतिम् ।
सेनानीनामहं स्कन्दः सरसामस्मि सागरः ॥ १०-२४ ॥
महर्षीणां भृगुरहं गिरामस्म्येकमक्षरम् ।
यज्ञानां जपयज्ञोऽस्मि स्थावराणां हिमालयः ॥ १०-२५ ॥
अश्वत्थः सर्ववृक्षाणां देवर्षीणां च नारदः ।
गन्धर्वाणां चित्ररथः सिद्धानां कपिलो मुनिः ॥ १०-२६ ॥
उच्चैःश्रवसमश्वानां विद्धि माममृतोद्भवम् ।
ऐरावतं गजेन्द्राणां नराणां च नराधिपम् ॥ १०-२७ ॥
आयुधानामहं वज्रं धेनूनामस्मि कामधुक् ।
प्रजनश्चास्मि कन्दर्पः सर्पाणामस्मि वासुकिः ॥ १०-२८ ॥
अनन्तश्चास्मि नागानां वरुणो यादसामहम् ।
पितॄणामर्यमा चास्मि यमः संयमतामहम् ॥ १०-२९ ॥
प्रह्लादश्चास्मि दैत्यानां कालः कलयतामहम् ।
मृगाणां च मृगेन्द्रोऽहं वैनतेयश्च पक्षिणाम् ॥ १०-३० ॥
पवनः पवतामस्मि रामः शस्त्रभृतामहम् ।
झषाणां मकरश्चास्मि स्रोतसामस्मि जाह्नवी ॥ १०-३१ ॥
सर्गाणामादिरन्तश्च मध्यं चैवाहमर्जुन ।
अध्यात्मविद्या विद्यानां वादः प्रवदतामहम् ॥ १०-३२ ॥
अक्षराणामकारोऽस्मि द्वन्द्वः सामासिकस्य च ।
अहमेवाक्षयः कालो धाताहं विश्वतोमुखः ॥ १०-३३ ॥
मृत्युः सर्वहरश्चाहमुद्भवश्च भविष्यताम् ।
कीर्तिः श्रीर्वाक्च नारीणां स्मृतिर्मेधा धृतिः क्षमा ॥ १०-३४ ॥
बृहत्साम तथा साम्नां गायत्री छन्दसामहम् ।
मासानां मार्गशीर्षोऽहमृतूनां कुसुमाकरः ॥ १०-३५ ॥
द्यूतं छलयतामस्मि तेजस्तेजस्विनामहम् ।
जयोऽस्मि व्यवसायोऽस्मि सत्त्वं सत्त्ववतामहम् ॥ १०-३६ ॥
वृष्णीनां वासुदेवोऽस्मि पाण्डवानां धनञ्जयः ।
मुनीनामप्यहं व्यासः कवीनामुशना कविः ॥ १०-३७ ॥
दण्डो दमयतामस्मि नीतिरस्मि जिगीषताम् ।
मौनं चैवास्मि गुह्यानां ज्ञानं ज्ञानवतामहम् ॥ १०-३८ ॥
यच्चापि सर्वभूतानां बीजं तदहमर्जुन ।
न तदस्ति विना यत्स्यान्मया भूतं चराचरम् ॥ १०-३९ ॥
नान्तोऽस्ति मम दिव्यानां विभूतीनां परन्तप ।
एष तूद्देशतः प्रोक्तो विभूतेर्विस्तरो मया ॥ १०-४० ॥
यद्यद्विभूतिमत्सत्त्वं श्रीमदूर्जितमेव वा ।
तत्तदेवावगच्छ त्वं मम तेजोंऽशसम्भवम् ॥ १०-४१ ॥
अथवा बहुनैतेन किं ज्ञातेन तवार्जुन ।
विष्टभ्याहमिदं कृत्स्नमेकांशेन स्थितो जगत् ॥ १०-४२ ॥

ॐ तत्सदिति श्रीमद्भगवद्गीतासूपनिषत्सु
ब्रह्मविद्यायां योगशास्त्रे श्रीकृष्णार्जुनसंवादे
विभूतियोगो नाम दशमोऽध्यायः ॥

एकादशोऽध्यायः - विश्वरूपदर्शनयोगः

अर्जुन उवाच –

मदनुग्रहाय परमं गुह्यमध्यात्मसंज्ञितम् ।
यत्त्वयोक्तं वचस्तेन मोहोऽयं विगतो मम ॥ ११-१ ॥
भवाप्ययौ हि भूतानां श्रुतौ विस्तरशो मया ।
त्वत्तः कमलपत्राक्ष माहात्म्यमपि चाव्ययम् ॥ ११-२ ॥
एवमेतद्यथात्थ त्वमात्मानं परमेश्वर ।
द्रष्टुमिच्छामि ते रूपमैश्वरं पुरुषोत्तम ॥ ११-३ ॥
मन्यसे यदि तच्छक्यं मया द्रष्टुमिति प्रभो ।
योगेश्वर ततो मे त्वं दर्शयात्मानमव्ययम् ॥ ११-४ ॥

श्रीभगवानुवाच –

पश्य मे पार्थ रूपाणि शतशोऽथ सहस्रशः ।
नानाविधानि दिव्यानि नानावर्णाकृतीनि च ॥ ११-५ ॥
पश्यादित्यान्वसून्रुद्रानश्विनौ मरुतस्तथा ।
बहून्यदृष्टपूर्वाणि पश्याश्चर्याणि भारत ॥ ११-६ ॥
इहैकस्थं जगत्कृत्स्नं पश्याद्य सचराचरम् ।
मम देहे गुडाकेश यच्चान्यद्द्रष्टुमिच्छसि ॥ ११-७ ॥
न तु मां शक्यसे द्रष्टुमनेनैव स्वचक्षुषा ।
दिव्यं ददामि ते चक्षुः पश्य मे योगमैश्वरम् ॥ ११-८ ॥

सञ्जय उवाच –

एवमुक्त्वा ततो राजन्महायोगेश्वरो हरिः ।
दर्शयामास पार्थाय परमं रूपमैश्वरम् ॥ ११-९ ॥
अनेकवक्त्रनयनमनेकाद्भुतदर्शनम् ।
अनेकदिव्याभरणं दिव्यानेकोद्यतायुधम् ॥ ११-१० ॥
दिव्यमाल्याम्बरधरं दिव्यगन्धानुलेपनम् ।
सर्वाश्चर्यमयं देवमनन्तं विश्वतोमुखम् ॥ ११-११ ॥
दिवि सूर्यसहस्रस्य भवेद्युगपदुत्थिता ।
यदि भाः सदृशी सा स्याद्भासस्तस्य महात्मनः ॥ ११-१२ ॥
तत्रैकस्थं जगत्कृत्स्नं प्रविभक्तमनेकधा ।
अपश्यद्देवदेवस्य शरीरे पाण्डवस्तदा ॥ ११-१३ ॥
ततः स विस्मयाविष्टो हृष्टरोमा धनञ्जयः ।
प्रणम्य शिरसा देवं कृताञ्जलिरभाषत ॥ ११-१४ ॥

अर्जुन उवाच –

पश्यामि देवांस्तव देव देहे सर्वांस्तथा भूतविशेषसङ्घान् ।
ब्रह्माणमीशं कमलासनस्थमृषींश्च सर्वानुरगांश्च दिव्यान् ॥ ११-१५ ॥
अनेकबाहूदरवक्त्रनेत्रं पश्यामि त्वां सर्वतोऽनन्तरूपम् ।
नान्तं न मध्यं न पुनस्तवादिं पश्यामि विश्वेश्वर विश्वरूप ॥ ११-१६ ॥
किरीटिनं गदिनं चक्रिणं च तेजोराशिं सर्वतो दीप्तिमन्तम् ।
पश्यामि त्वां दुर्निरीक्ष्यं समन्ताद्दीप्तानलार्कद्युतिमप्रमेयम् ॥ ११-१७ ॥
त्वमक्षरं परमं वेदितव्यं त्वमस्य विश्वस्य परं निधानम् ।
त्वमव्ययः शाश्वतधर्मगोप्ता सनातनस्त्वं पुरुषो मतो मे ॥ ११-१८ ॥
अनादिमध्यान्तमनन्तवीर्यमनन्तबाहुं शशिसूर्यनेत्रम् ।
पश्यामि त्वां दीप्तहुताशवक्त्रं स्वतेजसा विश्वमिदं तपन्तम् ॥ ११-१९ ॥
द्यावापृथिव्योरिदमन्तरं हि व्याप्तं त्वयैकेन दिशश्च सर्वाः ।
दृष्ट्वाद्भुतं रूपमुग्रं तवेदं लोकत्रयं प्रव्यथितं महात्मन् ॥ ११-२० ॥
अमी हि त्वां सुरसङ्घा विशन्ति केचिद्भीताः प्राञ्जलयो गृणन्ति ।
स्वस्तीत्युक्त्वा महर्षिसिद्धसङ्घाः स्तुवन्ति त्वां स्तुतिभिः पुष्कलाभिः ॥ ११-२१ ॥
रुद्रादित्या वसवो ये च साध्या विश्वेऽश्विनौ मरुतश्चोष्मपाश्च ।
गन्धर्वयक्षासुरसिद्धसङ्घा वीक्षन्ते त्वां विस्मिताश्चैव सर्वे ॥ ११-२२ ॥
रूपं महत्ते बहुवक्त्रनेत्रं महाबाहो बहुबाहूरुपादम् ।
बहूदरं बहुदंष्ट्राकरालं दृष्ट्वा लोकाः प्रव्यथितास्तथाहम् ॥ ११-२३ ॥
नभःस्पृशं दीप्तमनेकवर्णं व्यात्ताननं दीप्तविशालनेत्रम् ।
दृष्ट्वा हि त्वां प्रव्यथितान्तरात्मा धृतिं न विन्दामि शमं च विष्णो ॥ ११-२४ ॥
दंष्ट्राकरालानि च ते मुखानि दृष्ट्वैव कालानलसन्निभानि ।
दिशो न जाने न लभे च शर्म प्रसीद देवेश जगन्निवास ॥ ११-२५ ॥
अमी च त्वां धृतराष्ट्रस्य पुत्राः सर्वे सहैवावनिपालसङ्घैः ।
भीष्मो द्रोणः सूतपुत्रस्तथासौ सहास्मदीयैरपि योधमुख्यैः ॥ ११-२६ ॥
वक्त्राणि ते त्वरमाणा विशन्ति दंष्ट्राकरालानि भयानकानि ।
केचिद्विलग्ना दशनान्तरेषु सन्दृश्यन्ते चूर्णितैरुत्तमाङ्गैः ॥ ११-२७ ॥
यथा नदीनां बहवोऽम्बुवेगाः समुद्रमेवाभिमुखा द्रवन्ति ।
तथा तवामी नरलोकवीरा विशन्ति वक्त्राण्यभिविज्वलन्ति ॥ ११-२८ ॥
यथा प्रदीप्तं ज्वलनं पतङ्गा विशन्ति नाशाय समृद्धवेगाः ।
तथैव नाशाय विशन्ति लोकास्तवापि वक्त्राणि समृद्धवेगाः ॥ ११-२९ ॥
लेलिह्यसे ग्रसमानः समन्ताल्लोकान्समग्रान्वदनैर्ज्वलद्भिः ।
तेजोभिरापूर्य जगत्समग्रं भासस्तवोग्राः प्रतपन्ति विष्णो ॥ ११-३० ॥
आख्याहि मे को भवानुग्ररूपो नमोऽस्तु ते देववर प्रसीद ।
विज्ञातुमिच्छामि भवन्तमाद्यं न हि प्रजानामि तव प्रवृत्तिम् ॥ ११-३१ ॥

श्रीभगवानुवाच –

कालोऽस्मि लोकक्षयकृत्प्रवृद्धो लोकान्समाहर्तुमिह प्रवृत्तः ।
ऋतेऽपि त्वां न भविष्यन्ति सर्वे येऽवस्थिताः प्रत्यनीकेषु योधाः ॥ ११-३२ ॥
तस्मात्त्वमुत्तिष्ठ यशो लभस्व जित्वा शत्रून्भुङ्क्ष्व राज्यं समृद्धम् ।
मयैवैते निहताः पूर्वमेव निमित्तमात्रं भव सव्यसाचिन् ॥ ११-३३ ॥
द्रोणं च भीष्मं च जयद्रथं च कर्णं तथान्यानपि योधवीरान् ।
मया हतांस्त्वं जहि मा व्यथिष्ठा युध्यस्व जेतासि रणे सपत्नान् ॥ ११-३४ ॥

सञ्जय उवाच –

एतच्छ्रुत्वा वचनं केशवस्य कृताञ्जलिर्वेपमानः किरीटी ।
नमस्कृत्वा भूय एवाह कृष्णं सगद्गदं भीतभीतः प्रणम्य ॥ ११-३५ ॥

अर्जुन उवाच –

स्थाने हृषीकेश तव प्रकीर्त्या जगत्प्रहृष्यत्यनुरज्यते च ।
रक्षांसि भीतानि दिशो द्रवन्ति सर्वे नमस्यन्ति च सिद्धसङ्घाः ॥ ११-३६ ॥
कस्माच्च ते न नमेरन्महात्मन् गरीयसे ब्रह्मणोऽप्यादिकर्त्रे ।
अनन्त देवेश जगन्निवास त्वमक्षरं सदसत्तत्परं यत् ॥ ११-३७ ॥
त्वमादिदेवः पुरुषः पुराणस्त्वमस्य विश्वस्य परं निधानम् ।
वेत्तासि वेद्यं च परं च धाम त्वया ततं विश्वमनन्तरूप ॥ ११-३८ ॥
वायुर्यमोऽग्निर्वरुणः शशाङ्कः प्रजापतिस्त्वं प्रपितामहश्च ।
नमो नमस्तेऽस्तु सहस्रकृत्वः पुनश्च भूयोऽपि नमो नमस्ते ॥ ११-३९ ॥
नमः पुरस्तादथ पृष्ठतस्ते नमोऽस्तु ते सर्वत एव सर्व ।
अनन्तवीर्यामितविक्रमस्त्वं सर्वं समाप्नोषि ततोऽसि सर्वः ॥ ११-४० ॥
सखेति मत्वा प्रसभं यदुक्तं हे कृष्ण हे यादव हे सखेति ।
अजानता महिमानं तवेदं मया प्रमादात्प्रणयेन वापि ॥ ११-४१ ॥
यच्चावहासार्थमसत्कृतोऽसि विहारशय्यासनभोजनेषु ।
एकोऽथवाप्यच्युत तत्समक्षं तत्क्षामये त्वामहमप्रमेयम् ॥ ११-४२ ॥
पितासि लोकस्य चराचरस्य त्वमस्य पूज्यश्च गुरुर्गरीयान् ।
न त्वत्समोऽस्त्यभ्यधिकः कुतोऽन्यो लोकत्रयेऽप्यप्रतिमप्रभाव ॥ ११-४३ ॥
तस्मात्प्रणम्य प्रणिधाय कायं प्रसादये त्वामहमीशमीड्यम् ।
पितेव पुत्रस्य सखेव सख्युः प्रियः प्रियायार्हसि देव सोढुम् ॥ ११-४४ ॥
अदृष्टपूर्वं हृषितोऽस्मि दृष्ट्वा भयेन च प्रव्यथितं मनो मे ।
तदेव मे दर्शय देव रूपं प्रसीद देवेश जगन्निवास ॥ ११-४५ ॥
किरीटिनं गदिनं चक्रहस्तमिच्छामि त्वां द्रष्टुमहं तथैव ।
तेनैव रूपेण चतुर्भुजेन सहस्रबाहो भव विश्वमूर्ते ॥ ११-४६ ॥

श्रीभगवानुवाच –

मया प्रसन्नेन तवार्जुनेदं रूपं परं दर्शितमात्मयोगात् ।
तेजोमयं विश्वमनन्तमाद्यं यन्मे त्वदन्येन न दृष्टपूर्वम् ॥ ११-४७ ॥
न वेदयज्ञाध्ययनैर्न दानैर्न च क्रियाभिर्न तपोभिरुग्रैः ।
एवंरूपः शक्य अहं नृलोके द्रष्टुं त्वदन्येन कुरुप्रवीर ॥ ११-४८ ॥
मा ते व्यथा मा च विमूढभावो दृष्ट्वा रूपं घोरमीदृङ्ममेदम् ।
व्यपेतभीः प्रीतमनाः पुनस्त्वं तदेव मे रूपमिदं प्रपश्य ॥ ११-४९ ॥

सञ्जय उवाच –

इत्यर्जुनं वासुदेवस्तथोक्त्वा स्वकं रूपं दर्शयामास भूयः ।
आश्वासयामास च भीतमेनं भूत्वा पुनः सौम्यवपुर्महात्मा ॥ ११-५० ॥

अर्जुन उवाच –

दृष्ट्वेदं मानुषं रूपं तव सौम्यं जनार्दन ।
इदानीमस्मि संवृत्तः सचेताः प्रकृतिं गतः ॥ ११-५१ ॥

श्रीभगवानुवाच –

सुदुर्दर्शमिदं रूपं दृष्टवानसि यन्मम ।
देवा अप्यस्य रूपस्य नित्यं दर्शनकाङ्क्षिणः ॥ ११-५२ ॥
नाहं वेदैर्न तपसा न दानेन न चेज्यया ।
शक्य एवंविधो द्रष्टुं दृष्टवानसि मां यथा ॥ ११-५३ ॥
भक्त्या त्वनन्यया शक्य अहमेवंविधोऽर्जुन ।
ज्ञातुं द्रष्टुं च तत्त्वेन प्रवेष्टुं च परन्तप ॥ ११-५४ ॥
मत्कर्मकृन्मत्परमो मद्भक्तः सङ्गवर्जितः ।
निर्वैरः सर्वभूतेषु यः स मामेति पाण्डव ॥ ११-५५ ॥

ॐ तत्सदिति श्रीमद्भगवद्गीतासूपनिषत्सु
ब्रह्मविद्यायां योगशास्त्रे श्रीकृष्णार्जुनसंवादे
विश्वरूपदर्शनयोगो नामैकादशोऽध्यायः ॥

द्वादशोऽध्यायः - भक्तियोगः

अर्जुन उवाच –

एवं सततयुक्ता ये भक्तास्त्वां पर्युपासते ।
ये चाप्यक्षरमव्यक्तं तेषां के योगवित्तमाः ॥ १२-१ ॥

श्रीभगवानुवाच –

मय्यावेश्य मनो ये मां नित्ययुक्ता उपासते ।
श्रद्धया परयोपेतास्ते मे युक्ततमा मताः ॥ १२-२ ॥
ये त्वक्षरमनिर्देश्यमव्यक्तं पर्युपासते ।
सर्वत्रगमचिन्त्यं च कूटस्थमचलं ध्रुवम् ॥ १२-३ ॥
सन्नियम्येन्द्रियग्रामं सर्वत्र समबुद्धयः ।
ते प्राप्नुवन्ति मामेव सर्वभूतहिते रताः ॥ १२-४ ॥
क्लेशोऽधिकतरस्तेषामव्यक्तासक्तचेतसाम् ।
अव्यक्ता हि गतिर्दुःखं देहवद्भिरवाप्यते ॥ १२-५ ॥
ये तु सर्वाणि कर्माणि मयि संन्यस्य मत्पराः ।
अनन्येनैव योगेन मां ध्यायन्त उपासते ॥ १२-६ ॥
तेषामहं समुद्धर्ता मृत्युसंसारसागरात् ।
भवामि नचिरात्पार्थ मय्यावेशितचेतसाम् ॥ १२-७ ॥
मय्येव मन आधत्स्व मयि बुद्धिं निवेशय ।
निवसिष्यसि मय्येव अत ऊर्ध्वं न संशयः ॥ १२-८ ॥
अथ चित्तं समाधातुं न शक्नोषि मयि स्थिरम् ।
अभ्यासयोगेन ततो मामिच्छाप्तुं धनञ्जय ॥ १२-९ ॥
अभ्यासेऽप्यसमर्थोऽसि मत्कर्मपरमो भव ।
मदर्थमपि कर्माणि कुर्वन्सिद्धिमवाप्स्यसि ॥ १२-१० ॥
अथैतदप्यशक्तोऽसि कर्तुं मद्योगमाश्रितः ।
सर्वकर्मफलत्यागं ततः कुरु यतात्मवान् ॥ १२-११ ॥
श्रेयो हि ज्ञानमभ्यासाज्ज्ञानाद्ध्यानं विशिष्यते ।
ध्यानात्कर्मफलत्यागस्त्यागाच्छान्तिरनन्तरम् ॥ १२-१२ ॥
अद्वेष्टा सर्वभूतानां मैत्रः करुण एव च ।
निर्ममो निरहङ्कारः समदुःखसुखः क्षमी ॥ १२-१३ ॥
सन्तुष्टः सततं योगी यतात्मा दृढनिश्चयः ।
मय्यर्पितमनोबुद्धिर्यो मद्भक्तः स मे प्रियः ॥ १२-१४ ॥
यस्मान्नोद्विजते लोको लोकान्नोद्विजते च यः ।
हर्षामर्षभयोद्वेगैर्मुक्तो यः स च मे प्रियः ॥ १२-१५ ॥
अनपेक्षः शुचिर्दक्ष उदासीनो गतव्यथः ।
सर्वारम्भपरित्यागी यो मद्भक्तः स मे प्रियः ॥ १२-१६ ॥
यो न हृष्यति न द्वेष्टि न शोचति न काङ्क्षति ।
शुभाशुभपरित्यागी भक्तिमान्यः स मे प्रियः ॥ १२-१७ ॥
समः शत्रौ च मित्रे च तथा मानापमानयोः ।
शीतोष्णसुखदुःखेषु समः सङ्गविवर्जितः ॥ १२-१८ ॥
तुल्यनिन्दास्तुतिर्मौनी सन्तुष्टो येन केनचित् ।
अनिकेतः स्थिरमतिर्भक्तिमान्मे प्रियो नरः ॥ १२-१९ ॥
ये तु धर्म्यामृतमिदं यथोक्तं पर्युपासते ।
श्रद्दधाना मत्परमा भक्तास्तेऽतीव मे प्रियाः ॥ १२-२० ॥

ॐ तत्सदिति श्रीमद्भगवद्गीतासूपनिषत्सु
ब्रह्मविद्यायां योगशास्त्रे श्रीकृष्णार्जुनसंवादे
भक्तियोगो नाम द्वादशोऽध्यायः ॥

त्रयोदशोऽध्यायः - क्षेत्रक्षेत्रज्ञविभागयोगः

श्रीभगवानुवाच –

इदं शरीरं कौन्तेय क्षेत्रमित्यभिधीयते ।
एतद्यो वेत्ति तं प्राहुः क्षेत्रज्ञ इति तद्विदः ॥ १३-१ ॥
क्षेत्रज्ञं चापि मां विद्धि सर्वक्षेत्रेषु भारत ।
क्षेत्रक्षेत्रज्ञयोर्ज्ञानं यत्तज्ज्ञानं मतं मम ॥ १३-२ ॥
तत्क्षेत्रं यच्च यादृक्च यद्विकारि यतश्च यत् ।
स च यो यत्प्रभावश्च तत्समासेन मे शृणु ॥ १३-३ ॥
ऋषिभिर्बहुधा गीतं छन्दोभिर्विविधैः पृथक् ।
ब्रह्मसूत्रपदैश्चैव हेतुमद्भिर्विनिश्चितैः ॥ १३-४ ॥
महाभूतान्यहङ्कारो बुद्धिरव्यक्तमेव च ।
इन्द्रियाणि दशैकं च पञ्च चेन्द्रियगोचराः ॥ १३-५ ॥
इच्छा द्वेषः सुखं दुःखं सङ्घातश्चेतना धृतिः ।
एतत्क्षेत्रं समासेन सविकारमुदाहृतम् ॥ १३-६ ॥
अमानित्वमदम्भित्वमहिंसा क्षान्तिरार्जवम् ।
आचार्योपासनं शौचं स्थैर्यमात्मविनिग्रहः ॥ १३-७ ॥
इन्द्रियार्थेषु वैराग्यमनहङ्कार एव च ।
जन्ममृत्युजराव्याधिदुःखदोषानुदर्शनम् ॥ १३-८ ॥
असक्तिरनभिष्वङ्गः पुत्रदारगृहादिषु ।
नित्यं च समचित्तत्वमिष्टानिष्टोपपत्तिषु ॥ १३-९ ॥
मयि चानन्ययोगेन भक्तिरव्यभिचारिणी ।
विविक्तदेशसेवित्वमरतिर्जनसंसदि ॥ १३-१० ॥
अध्यात्मज्ञाननित्यत्वं तत्त्वज्ञानार्थदर्शनम् ।
एतज्ज्ञानमिति प्रोक्तमज्ञानं यदतोऽन्यथा ॥ १३-११ ॥
ज्ञेयं यत्तत्प्रवक्ष्यामि यज्ज्ञात्वामृतमश्नुते ।
अनादिमत्परं ब्रह्म न सत्तन्नासदुच्यते ॥ १३-१२ ॥
सर्वतः पाणिपादं तत्सर्वतोऽक्षिशिरोमुखम् ।
सर्वतः श्रुतिमल्लोके सर्वमावृत्य तिष्ठति ॥ १३-१३ ॥
सर्वेन्द्रियगुणाभासं सर्वेन्द्रियविवर्जितम् ।
असक्तं सर्वभृच्चैव निर्गुणं गुणभोक्तृ च ॥ १३-१४ ॥
बहिरन्तश्च भूतानामचरं चरमेव च ।
सूक्ष्मत्वात्तदविज्ञेयं दूरस्थं चान्तिके च तत् ॥ १३-१५ ॥
अविभक्तं च भूतेषु विभक्तमिव च स्थितम् ।
भूतभर्तृ च तज्ज्ञेयं ग्रसिष्णु प्रभविष्णु च ॥ १३-१६ ॥
ज्योतिषामपि तज्ज्योतिस्तमसः परमुच्यते ।
ज्ञानं ज्ञेयं ज्ञानगम्यं हृदि सर्वस्य विष्ठितम् ॥ १३-१७ ॥
इति क्षेत्रं तथा ज्ञानं ज्ञेयं चोक्तं समासतः ।
मद्भक्त एतद्विज्ञाय मद्भावायोपपद्यते ॥ १३-१८ ॥
प्रकृतिं पुरुषं चैव विद्ध्यनादी उभावपि ।
विकारांश्च गुणांश्चैव विद्धि प्रकृतिसम्भवान् ॥ १३-१९ ॥
कार्यकारणकर्तृत्वे हेतुः प्रकृतिरुच्यते ।
पुरुषः सुखदुःखानां भोक्तृत्वे हेतुरुच्यते ॥ १३-२० ॥
पुरुषः प्रकृतिस्थो हि भुङ्क्ते प्रकृतिजान्गुणान् ।
कारणं गुणसङ्गोऽस्य सदसद्योनिजन्मसु ॥ १३-२१ ॥
उपद्रष्टानुमन्ता च भर्ता भोक्ता महेश्वरः ।
परमात्मेति चाप्युक्तो देहेऽस्मिन्पुरुषः परः ॥ १३-२२ ॥
य एवं वेत्ति पुरुषं प्रकृतिं च गुणैः सह ।
सर्वथा वर्तमानोऽपि न स भूयोऽभिजायते ॥ १३-२३ ॥
ध्यानेनात्मनि पश्यन्ति केचिदात्मानमात्मना ।
अन्ये साङ्ख्येन योगेन कर्मयोगेन चापरे ॥ १३-२४ ॥
अन्ये त्वेवमजानन्तः श्रुत्वान्येभ्य उपासते ।
तेऽपि चातितरन्त्येव मृत्युं श्रुतिपरायणाः ॥ १३-२५ ॥
यावत्सञ्जायते किञ्चित्सत्त्वं स्थावरजङ्गमम् ।
क्षेत्रक्षेत्रज्ञसंयोगात्तद्विद्धि भरतर्षभ ॥ १३-२६ ॥
समं सर्वेषु भूतेषु तिष्ठन्तं परमेश्वरम् ।
विनश्यत्स्वविनश्यन्तं यः पश्यति स पश्यति ॥ १३-२७ ॥
समं पश्यन्हि सर्वत्र समवस्थितमीश्वरम् ।
न हिनस्त्यात्मनात्मानं ततो याति परां गतिम् ॥ १३-२८ ॥
प्रकृत्यैव च कर्माणि क्रियमाणानि सर्वशः ।
यः पश्यति तथात्मानमकर्तारं स पश्यति ॥ १३-२९ ॥
यदा भूतपृथग्भावमेकस्थमनुपश्यति ।
तत एव च विस्तारं ब्रह्म सम्पद्यते तदा ॥ १३-३० ॥
अनादित्वान्निर्गुणत्वात्परमात्मायमव्ययः ।
शरीरस्थोऽपि कौन्तेय न करोति न लिप्यते ॥ १३-३१ ॥
यथा सर्वगतं सौक्ष्म्यादाकाशं नोपलिप्यते ।
सर्वत्रावस्थितो देहे तथात्मा नोपलिप्यते ॥ १३-३२ ॥
यथा प्रकाशयत्येकः कृत्स्नं लोकमिमं रविः ।
क्षेत्रं क्षेत्री तथा कृत्स्नं प्रकाशयति भारत ॥ १३-३३ ॥
क्षेत्रक्षेत्रज्ञयोरेवमन्तरं ज्ञानचक्षुषा ।
भूतप्रकृतिमोक्षं च ये विदुर्यान्ति ते परम् ॥ १३-३४ ॥

ॐ तत्सदिति श्रीमद्भगवद्गीतासूपनिषत्सु
ब्रह्मविद्यायां योगशास्त्रे श्रीकृष्णार्जुनसंवादे
क्षेत्रक्षेत्रज्ञविभागयोगो नाम त्रयोदशोऽध्यायः ॥

चतुर्दशोऽध्यायः - गुणत्रयविभागयोगः

श्रीभगवानुवाच –

परं भूयः प्रवक्ष्यामि ज्ञानानां ज्ञानमुत्तमम् ।
यज्ज्ञात्वा मुनयः सर्वे परां सिद्धिमितो गताः ॥ १४-१ ॥
इदं ज्ञानमुपाश्रित्य मम साधर्म्यमागताः ।
सर्गेऽपि नोपजायन्ते प्रलये न व्यथन्ति च ॥ १४-२ ॥
मम योनिर्महद्ब्रह्म तस्मिन्गर्भं दधाम्यहम् ।
सम्भवः सर्वभूतानां ततो भवति भारत ॥ १४-३ ॥
सर्वयोनिषु कौन्तेय मूर्तयः सम्भवन्ति याः ।
तासां ब्रह्म महद्योनिरहं बीजप्रदः पिता ॥ १४-४ ॥
सत्त्वं रजस्तम इति गुणाः प्रकृतिसम्भवाः ।
निबध्नन्ति महाबाहो देहे देहिनमव्ययम् ॥ १४-५ ॥
तत्र सत्त्वं निर्मलत्वात्प्रकाशकमनामयम् ।
सुखसङ्गेन बध्नाति ज्ञानसङ्गेन चानघ ॥ १४-६ ॥
रजो रागात्मकं विद्धि तृष्णासङ्गसमुद्भवम् ।
तन्निबध्नाति कौन्तेय कर्मसङ्गेन देहिनम् ॥ १४-७ ॥
तमस्त्वज्ञानजं विद्धि मोहनं सर्वदेहिनाम् ।
प्रमादालस्यनिद्राभिस्तन्निबध्नाति भारत ॥ १४-८ ॥
सत्त्वं सुखे सञ्जयति रजः कर्मणि भारत ।
ज्ञानमावृत्य तु तमः प्रमादे सञ्जयत्युत ॥ १४-९ ॥
रजस्तमश्चाभिभूय सत्त्वं भवति भारत ।
रजः सत्त्वं तमश्चैव तमः सत्त्वं रजस्तथा ॥ १४-१० ॥
सर्वद्वारेषु देहेऽस्मिन्प्रकाश उपजायते ।
ज्ञानं यदा तदा विद्याद्विवृद्धं सत्त्वमित्युत ॥ १४-११ ॥
लोभः प्रवृत्तिरारम्भः कर्मणामशमः स्पृहा ।
रजस्येतानि जायन्ते विवृद्धे भरतर्षभ ॥ १४-१२ ॥
अप्रकाशोऽप्रवृत्तिश्च प्रमादो मोह एव च ।
तमस्येतानि जायन्ते विवृद्धे कुरुनन्दन ॥ १४-१३ ॥
यदा सत्त्वे प्रवृद्धे तु प्रलयं याति देहभृत् ।
तदोत्तमविदां लोकानमलान्प्रतिपद्यते ॥ १४-१४ ॥
रजसि प्रलयं गत्वा कर्मसङ्गिषु जायते ।
तथा प्रलीनस्तमसि मूढयोनिषु जायते ॥ १४-१५ ॥
कर्मणः सुकृतस्याहुः सात्त्विकं निर्मलं फलम् ।
रजसस्तु फलं दुःखमज्ञानं तमसः फलम् ॥ १४-१६ ॥
सत्त्वात्सञ्जायते ज्ञानं रजसो लोभ एव च ।
प्रमादमोहौ तमसो भवतोऽज्ञानमेव च ॥ १४-१७ ॥
ऊर्ध्वं गच्छन्ति सत्त्वस्था मध्ये तिष्ठन्ति राजसाः ।
जघन्यगुणवृत्तिस्था अधो गच्छन्ति तामसाः ॥ १४-१८ ॥
नान्यं गुणेभ्यः कर्तारं यदा द्रष्टानुपश्यति ।
गुणेभ्यश्च परं वेत्ति मद्भावं सोऽधिगच्छति ॥ १४-१९ ॥
गुणानेतानतीत्य त्रीन्देही देहसमुद्भवान् ।
जन्ममृत्युजरादुःखैर्विमुक्तोऽमृतमश्नुते ॥ १४-२० ॥

अर्जुन उवाच –

कैर्लिङ्गैस्त्रीन्गुणानेतानतीतो भवति प्रभो ।
किमाचारः कथं चैतांस्त्रीन्गुणानतिवर्तते ॥ १४-२१ ॥

श्रीभगवानुवाच –

प्रकाशं च प्रवृत्तिं च मोहमेव च पाण्डव ।
न द्वेष्टि सम्प्रवृत्तानि न निवृत्तानि काङ्क्षति ॥ १४-२२ ॥
उदासीनवदासीनो गुणैर्यो न विचाल्यते ।
गुणा वर्तन्त इत्येव योऽवतिष्ठति नेङ्गते ॥ १४-२३ ॥
समदुःखसुखः स्वस्थः समलोष्टाश्मकाञ्चनः ।
तुल्यप्रियाप्रियो धीरस्तुल्यनिन्दात्मसंस्तुतिः ॥ १४-२४ ॥
मानापमानयोस्तुल्यस्तुल्यो मित्रारिपक्षयोः ।
सर्वारम्भपरित्यागी गुणातीतः स उच्यते ॥ १४-२५ ॥
मां च योऽव्यभिचारेण भक्तियोगेन सेवते ।
स गुणान्समतीत्यैतान्ब्रह्मभूयाय कल्पते ॥ १४-२६ ॥
ब्रह्मणो हि प्रतिष्ठाहममृतस्याव्ययस्य च ।
शाश्वतस्य च धर्मस्य सुखस्यैकान्तिकस्य च ॥ १४-२७ ॥

ॐ तत्सदिति श्रीमद्भगवद्गीतासूपनिषत्सु
ब्रह्मविद्यायां योगशास्त्रे श्रीकृष्णार्जुनसंवादे
गुणत्रयविभागयोगो नाम चतुर्दशोऽध्यायः ॥

पञ्चदशोऽध्यायः - पुरुषोत्तमयोगः

श्रीभगवानुवाच –

ऊर्ध्वमूलमधःशाखमश्वत्थं प्राहुरव्ययम् ।
छन्दांसि यस्य पर्णानि यस्तं वेद स वेदवित् ॥ १५-१ ॥
अधश्चोर्ध्वं प्रसृतास्तस्य शाखा गुणप्रवृद्धा विषयप्रवालाः ।
अधश्च मूलान्यनुसन्ततानि कर्मानुबन्धीनि मनुष्यलोके ॥ १५-२ ॥
न रूपमस्येह तथोपलभ्यते नान्तो न चादिर्न च सम्प्रतिष्ठा ।
अश्वत्थमेनं सुविरूढमूलमसङ्गशस्त्रेण दृढेन छित्त्वा ॥ १५-३ ॥
ततः पदं तत्परिमार्गितव्यं यस्मिन्गता न निवर्तन्ति भूयः ।
तमेव चाद्यं पुरुषं प्रपद्ये यतः प्रवृत्तिः प्रसृता पुराणी ॥ १५-४ ॥
निर्मानमोहा जितसङ्गदोषा अध्यात्मनित्या विनिवृत्तकामाः ।
द्वन्द्वैर्विमुक्ताः सुखदुःखसंज्ञैर्गच्छन्त्यमूढाः पदमव्ययं तत् ॥ १५-५ ॥
न तद्भासयते सूर्यो न शशाङ्को न पावकः ।
यद्गत्वा न निवर्तन्ते तद्धाम परमं मम ॥ १५-६ ॥
ममैवांशो जीवलोके जीवभूतः सनातनः ।
मनःषष्ठानीन्द्रियाणि प्रकृतिस्थानि कर्षति ॥ १५-७ ॥
शरीरं यदवाप्नोति यच्चाप्युत्क्रामतीश्वरः ।
गृहीत्वैतानि संयाति वायुर्गन्धानिवाशयात् ॥ १५-८ ॥
श्रोत्रं चक्षुः स्पर्शनं च रसनं घ्राणमेव च ।
अधिष्ठाय मनश्चायं विषयानुपसेवते ॥ १५-९ ॥
उत्क्रामन्तं स्थितं वापि भुञ्जानं वा गुणान्वितम् ।
विमूढा नानुपश्यन्ति पश्यन्ति ज्ञानचक्षुषः ॥ १५-१० ॥
यतन्तो योगिनश्चैनं पश्यन्त्यात्मन्यवस्थितम् ।
यतन्तोऽप्यकृतात्मानो नैनं पश्यन्त्यचेतसः ॥ १५-११ ॥
यदादित्यगतं तेजो जगद्भासयतेऽखिलम् ।
यच्चन्द्रमसि यच्चाग्नौ तत्तेजो विद्धि मामकम् ॥ १५-१२ ॥
गामाविश्य च भूतानि धारयाम्यहमोजसा ।
पुष्णामि चौषधीः सर्वाः सोमो भूत्वा रसात्मकः ॥ १५-१३ ॥
अहं वैश्वानरो भूत्वा प्राणिनां देहमाश्रितः ।
प्राणापानसमायुक्तः पचाम्यन्नं चतुर्विधम् ॥ १५-१४ ॥
सर्वस्य चाहं हृदि सन्निविष्टो मत्तः स्मृतिर्ज्ञानमपोहनं च ।
वेदैश्च सर्वैरहमेव वेद्यो वेदान्तकृद्वेदविदेव चाहम् ॥ १५-१५ ॥
द्वाविमौ पुरुषौ लोके क्षरश्चाक्षर एव च ।
क्षरः सर्वाणि भूतानि कूटस्थोऽक्षर उच्यते ॥ १५-१६ ॥
उत्तमः पुरुषस्त्वन्यः परमात्मेत्युदाहृतः ।
यो लोकत्रयमाविश्य बिभर्त्यव्यय ईश्वरः ॥ १५-१७ ॥
यस्मात्क्षरमतीतोऽहमक्षरादपि चोत्तमः ।
अतोऽस्मि लोके वेदे च प्रथितः पुरुषोत्तमः ॥ १५-१८ ॥
यो मामेवमसम्मूढो जानाति पुरुषोत्तमम् ।
स सर्वविद्भजति मां सर्वभावेन भारत ॥ १५-१९ ॥
इति गुह्यतमं शास्त्रमिदमुक्तं मयानघ ।
एतद्बुद्ध्वा बुद्धिमान्स्यात्कृतकृत्यश्च भारत ॥ १५-२० ॥

ॐ तत्सदिति श्रीमद्भगवद्गीतासूपनिषत्सु
ब्रह्मविद्यायां योगशास्त्रे श्रीकृष्णार्जुनसंवादे
पुरुषोत्तमयोगो नाम पञ्चदशोऽध्यायः ॥

षोडशोऽध्यायः - दैवासुरसम्पद्विभागयोगः

श्रीभगवानुवाच –

अभयं सत्त्वसंशुद्धिर्ज्ञानयोगव्यवस्थितिः ।
दानं दमश्च यज्ञश्च स्वाध्यायस्तप आर्जवम् ॥ १६-१ ॥
अहिंसा सत्यमक्रोधस्त्यागः शान्तिरपैशुनम् ।
दया भूतेष्वलोलुप्त्वं मार्दवं ह्रीरचापलम् ॥ १६-२ ॥
तेजः क्षमा धृतिः शौचमद्रोहो नातिमानिता ।
भवन्ति सम्पदं दैवीमभिजातस्य भारत ॥ १६-३ ॥
दम्भो दर्पोऽभिमानश्च क्रोधः पारुष्यमेव च ।
अज्ञानं चाभिजातस्य पार्थ सम्पदमासुरीम् ॥ १६-४ ॥
दैवी सम्पद्विमोक्षाय निबन्धायासुरी मता ।
मा शुचः सम्पदं दैवीमभिजातोऽसि पाण्डव ॥ १६-५ ॥
द्वौ भूतसर्गौ लोकेऽस्मिन्दैव आसुर एव च ।
दैवो विस्तरशः प्रोक्त आसुरं पार्थ मे शृणु ॥ १६-६ ॥
प्रवृत्तिं च निवृत्तिं च जना न विदुरासुराः ।
न शौचं नापि चाचारो न सत्यं तेषु विद्यते ॥ १६-७ ॥
असत्यमप्रतिष्ठं ते जगदाहुरनीश्वरम् ।
अपरस्परसम्भूतं किमन्यत्कामहैतुकम् ॥ १६-८ ॥
एतां दृष्टिमवष्टभ्य नष्टात्मानोऽल्पबुद्धयः ।
प्रभवन्त्युग्रकर्माणः क्षयाय जगतोऽहिताः ॥ १६-९ ॥
काममाश्रित्य दुष्पूरं दम्भमानमदान्विताः ।
मोहाद्गृहीत्वासद्ग्राहान्प्रवर्तन्तेऽशुचिव्रताः ॥ १६-१० ॥
चिन्तामपरिमेयां च प्रलयान्तामुपाश्रिताः ।
कामोपभोगपरमा एतावदिति निश्चिताः ॥ १६-११ ॥
आशापाशशतैर्बद्धाः कामक्रोधपरायणाः ।
ईहन्ते कामभोगार्थमन्यायेनार्थसञ्चयान् ॥ १६-१२ ॥
इदमद्य मया लब्धमिमं प्राप्स्ये मनोरथम् ।
इदमस्तीदमपि मे भविष्यति पुनर्धनम् ॥ १६-१३ ॥
असौ मया हतः शत्रुर्हनिष्ये चापरानपि ।
ईश्वरोऽहमहं भोगी सिद्धोऽहं बलवान्सुखी ॥ १६-१४ ॥
आढ्योऽभिजनवानस्मि कोऽन्योऽस्ति सदृशो मया ।
यक्ष्ये दास्यामि मोदिष्य इत्यज्ञानविमोहिताः ॥ १६-१५ ॥
अनेकचित्तविभ्रान्ता मोहजालसमावृताः ।
प्रसक्ताः कामभोगेषु पतन्ति नरकेऽशुचौ ॥ १६-१६ ॥
आत्मसम्भाविताः स्तब्धा धनमानमदान्विताः ।
यजन्ते नामयज्ञैस्ते दम्भेनाविधिपूर्वकम् ॥ १६-१७ ॥
अहङ्कारं बलं दर्पं कामं क्रोधं च संश्रिताः ।
मामात्मपरदेहेषु प्रद्विषन्तोऽभ्यसूयकाः ॥ १६-१८ ॥
तानहं द्विषतः क्रूरान्संसारेषु नराधमान् ।
क्षिपाम्यजस्रमशुभानासुरीष्वेव योनिषु ॥ १६-१९ ॥
आसुरीं योनिमापन्ना मूढा जन्मनि जन्मनि ।
मामप्राप्यैव कौन्तेय ततो यान्त्यधमां गतिम् ॥ १६-२० ॥
त्रिविधं नरकस्येदं द्वारं नाशनमात्मनः ।
कामः क्रोधस्तथा लोभस्तस्मादेतत्त्रयं त्यजेत् ॥ १६-२१ ॥
एतैर्विमुक्तः कौन्तेय तमोद्वारैस्त्रिभिर्नरः ।
आचरत्यात्मनः श्रेयस्ततो याति परां गतिम् ॥ १६-२२ ॥
यः शास्त्रविधिमुत्सृज्य वर्तते कामकारतः ।
न स सिद्धिमवाप्नोति न सुखं न परां गतिम् ॥ १६-२३ ॥
तस्माच्छास्त्रं प्रमाणं ते कार्याकार्यव्यवस्थितौ ।
ज्ञात्वा शास्त्रविधानोक्तं कर्म कर्तुमिहार्हसि ॥ १६-२४ ॥

ॐ तत्सदिति श्रीमद्भगवद्गीतासूपनिषत्सु
ब्रह्मविद्यायां योगशास्त्रे श्रीकृष्णार्जुनसंवादे
दैवासुरसम्पद्विभागयोगो नाम षोडशोऽध्यायः ॥

सप्तदशोऽध्यायः - श्रद्धात्रयविभागयोगः

अर्जुन उवाच –

ये शास्त्रविधिमुत्सृज्य यजन्ते श्रद्धयान्विताः ।
तेषां निष्ठा तु का कृष्ण सत्त्वमाहो रजस्तमः ॥ १७-१ ॥

श्रीभगवानुवाच –

त्रिविधा भवति श्रद्धा देहिनां सा स्वभावजा ।
सात्त्विकी राजसी चैव तामसी चेति तां शृणु ॥ १७-२ ॥
सत्त्वानुरूपा सर्वस्य श्रद्धा भवति भारत ।
श्रद्धामयोऽयं पुरुषो यो यच्छ्रद्धः स एव सः ॥ १७-३ ॥
यजन्ते सात्त्विका देवान्यक्षरक्षांसि राजसाः ।
प्रेतान्भूतगणांश्चान्ये यजन्ते तामसा जनाः ॥ १७-४ ॥
अशास्त्रविहितं घोरं तप्यन्ते ये तपो जनाः ।
दम्भाहङ्कारसंयुक्ताः कामरागबलान्विताः ॥ १७-५ ॥
कर्षयन्तः शरीरस्थं भूतग्राममचेतसः ।
मां चैवान्तःशरीरस्थं तान्विद्ध्यासुरनिश्चयान् ॥ १७-६ ॥
आहारस्त्वपि सर्वस्य त्रिविधो भवति प्रियः ।
यज्ञस्तपस्तथा दानं तेषां भेदमिमं शृणु ॥ १७-७ ॥
आयुःसत्त्वबलारोग्यसुखप्रीतिविवर्धनाः ।
रस्याः स्निग्धाः स्थिरा हृद्या आहाराः सात्त्विकप्रियाः ॥ १७-८ ॥
कट्वम्ललवणात्युष्णतीक्ष्णरूक्षविदाहिनः ।
आहारा राजसस्येष्टा दुःखशोकामयप्रदाः ॥ १७-९ ॥
यातयामं गतरसं पूति पर्युषितं च यत् ।
उच्छिष्टमपि चामेध्यं भोजनं तामसप्रियम् ॥ १७-१० ॥
अफलाकाङ्क्षिभिर्यज्ञो विधिदृष्टो य इज्यते ।
यष्टव्यमेवेति मनः समाधाय स सात्त्विकः ॥ १७-११ ॥
अभिसन्धाय तु फलं दम्भार्थमपि चैव यत् ।
इज्यते भरतश्रेष्ठ तं यज्ञं विद्धि राजसम् ॥ १७-१२ ॥
विधिहीनमसृष्टान्नं मन्त्रहीनमदक्षिणम् ।
श्रद्धाविरहितं यज्ञं तामसं परिचक्षते ॥ १७-१३ ॥
देवद्विजगुरुप्राज्ञपूजनं शौचमार्जवम् ।
ब्रह्मचर्यमहिंसा च शारीरं तप उच्यते ॥ १७-१४ ॥
अनुद्वेगकरं वाक्यं सत्यं प्रियहितं च यत् ।
स्वाध्यायाभ्यसनं चैव वाङ्मयं तप उच्यते ॥ १७-१५ ॥
मनःप्रसादः सौम्यत्वं मौनमात्मविनिग्रहः ।
भावसंशुद्धिरित्येतत्तपो मानसमुच्यते ॥ १७-१६ ॥
श्रद्धया परया तप्तं तपस्तत्त्रिविधं नरैः ।
अफलाकाङ्क्षिभिर्युक्तैः सात्त्विकं परिचक्षते ॥ १७-१७ ॥
सत्कारमानपूजार्थं तपो दम्भेन चैव यत् ।
क्रियते तदिह प्रोक्तं राजसं चलमध्रुवम् ॥ १७-१८ ॥
मूढग्राहेणात्मनो यत्पीडया क्रियते तपः ।
परस्योत्सादनार्थं वा तत्तामसमुदाहृतम् ॥ १७-१९ ॥
दातव्यमिति यद्दानं दीयतेऽनुपकारिणे ।
देशे काले च पात्रे च तद्दानं सात्त्विकं स्मृतम् ॥ १७-२० ॥
यत्तु प्रत्युपकारार्थं फलमुद्दिश्य वा पुनः ।
दीयते च परिक्लिष्टं तद्दानं राजसं स्मृतम् ॥ १७-२१ ॥
अदेशकाले यद्दानमपात्रेभ्यश्च दीयते ।
असत्कृतमवज्ञातं तत्तामसमुदाहृतम् ॥ १७-२२ ॥
ॐ तत्सदिति निर्देशो ब्रह्मणस्त्रिविधः स्मृतः ।
ब्राह्मणास्तेन वेदाश्च यज्ञाश्च विहिताः पुरा ॥ १७-२३ ॥
तस्मादोमित्युदाहृत्य यज्ञदानतपःक्रियाः ।
प्रवर्तन्ते विधानोक्ताः सततं ब्रह्मवादिनाम् ॥ १७-२४ ॥
तदित्यनभिसन्धाय फलं यज्ञतपःक्रियाः ।
दानक्रियाश्च विविधाः क्रियन्ते मोक्षकाङ्क्षिभिः ॥ १७-२५ ॥
सद्भावे साधुभावे च सदित्येतत्प्रयुज्यते ।
प्रशस्ते कर्मणि तथा सच्छब्दः पार्थ युज्यते ॥ १७-२६ ॥
यज्ञे तपसि दाने च स्थितिः सदिति चोच्यते ।
कर्म चैव तदर्थीयं सदित्येवाभिधीयते ॥ १७-२७ ॥
अश्रद्धया हुतं दत्तं तपस्तप्तं कृतं च यत् ।
असदित्युच्यते पार्थ न च तत्प्रेत्य नो इह ॥ १७-२८ ॥

ॐ तत्सदिति श्रीमद्भगवद्गीतासूपनिषत्सु
ब्रह्मविद्यायां योगशास्त्रे श्रीकृष्णार्जुनसंवादे
श्रद्धात्रयविभागयोगो नाम सप्तदशोऽध्यायः ॥

अष्टादशोऽध्यायः - मोक्षसंन्यासयोगः

अर्जुन उवाच –

संन्यासस्य महाबाहो तत्त्वमिच्छामि वेदितुम् ।
त्यागस्य च हृषीकेश पृथक्केशिनिषूदन ॥ १८-१ ॥

श्रीभगवानुवाच –

काम्यानां कर्मणां न्यासं संन्यासं कवयो विदुः ।
सर्वकर्मफलत्यागं प्राहुस्त्यागं विचक्षणाः ॥ १८-२ ॥
त्याज्यं दोषवदित्येके कर्म प्राहुर्मनीषिणः ।
यज्ञदानतपःकर्म न त्याज्यमिति चापरे ॥ १८-३ ॥
निश्चयं शृणु मे तत्र त्यागे भरतसत्तम ।
त्यागो हि पुरुषव्याघ्र त्रिविधः सम्प्रकीर्तितः ॥ १८-४ ॥
यज्ञदानतपःकर्म न त्याज्यं कार्यमेव तत् ।
यज्ञो दानं तपश्चैव पावनानि मनीषिणाम् ॥ १८-५ ॥
एतान्यपि तु कर्माणि सङ्गं त्यक्त्वा फलानि च ।
कर्तव्यानीति मे पार्थ निश्चितं मतमुत्तमम् ॥ १८-६ ॥
नियतस्य तु संन्यासः कर्मणो नोपपद्यते ।
मोहात्तस्य परित्यागस्तामसः परिकीर्तितः ॥ १८-७ ॥
दुःखमित्येव यत्कर्म कायक्लेशभयात्त्यजेत् ।
स कृत्वा राजसं त्यागं नैव त्यागफलं लभेत् ॥ १८-८ ॥
कार्यमित्येव यत्कर्म नियतं क्रियतेऽर्जुन ।
सङ्गं त्यक्त्वा फलं चैव स त्यागः सात्त्विको मतः ॥ १८-९ ॥
न द्वेष्ट्यकुशलं कर्म कुशले नानुषज्जते ।
त्यागी सत्त्वसमाविष्टो मेधावी छिन्नसंशयः ॥ १८-१० ॥
न हि देहभृता शक्यं त्यक्तुं कर्माण्यशेषतः ।
यस्तु कर्मफलत्यागी स त्यागीत्यभिधीयते ॥ १८-११ ॥
अनिष्टमिष्टं मिश्रं च त्रिविधं कर्मणः फलम् ।
भवत्यत्यागिनां प्रेत्य न तु संन्यासिनां क्वचित् ॥ १८-१२ ॥
पञ्चैतानि महाबाहो कारणानि निबोध मे ।
साङ्ख्ये कृतान्ते प्रोक्तानि सिद्धये सर्वकर्मणाम् ॥ १८-१३ ॥
अधिष्ठानं तथा कर्ता करणं च पृथग्विधम् ।
विविधाश्च पृथक्चेष्टा दैवं चैवात्र पञ्चमम् ॥ १८-१४ ॥
शरीरवाङ्मनोभिर्यत्कर्म प्रारभते नरः ।
न्याय्यं वा विपरीतं वा पञ्चैते तस्य हेतवः ॥ १८-१५ ॥
तत्रैवं सति कर्तारमात्मानं केवलं तु यः ।
पश्यत्यकृतबुद्धित्वान्न स पश्यति दुर्मतिः ॥ १८-१६ ॥
यस्य नाहङ्कृतो भावो बुद्धिर्यस्य न लिप्यते ।
हत्वापि स इमाँल्लोकान्न हन्ति न निबध्यते ॥ १८-१७ ॥
ज्ञानं ज्ञेयं परिज्ञाता त्रिविधा कर्मचोदना ।
करणं कर्म कर्तेति त्रिविधः कर्मसङ्ग्रहः ॥ १८-१८ ॥
ज्ञानं कर्म च कर्ता च त्रिधैव गुणभेदतः ।
प्रोच्यते गुणसङ्ख्याने यथावच्छृणु तान्यपि ॥ १८-१९ ॥
सर्वभूतेषु येनैकं भावमव्ययमीक्षते ।
अविभक्तं विभक्तेषु तज्ज्ञानं विद्धि सात्त्विकम् ॥ १८-२० ॥
पृथक्त्वेन तु यज्ज्ञानं नानाभावान्पृथग्विधान् ।
वेत्ति सर्वेषु भूतेषु तज्ज्ञानं विद्धि राजसम् ॥ १८-२१ ॥
यत्तु कृत्स्नवदेकस्मिन्कार्ये सक्तमहैतुकम् ।
अतत्त्वार्थवदल्पं च तत्तामसमुदाहृतम् ॥ १८-२२ ॥
नियतं सङ्गरहितमरागद्वेषतः कृतम् ।
अफलप्रेप्सुना कर्म यत्तत्सात्त्विकमुच्यते ॥ १८-२३ ॥
यत्तु कामेप्सुना कर्म साहङ्कारेण वा पुनः ।
क्रियते बहुलायासं तद्राजसमुदाहृतम् ॥ १८-२४ ॥
अनुबन्धं क्षयं हिंसामनवेक्ष्य च पौरुषम् ।
मोहादारभ्यते कर्म यत्तत्तामसमुच्यते ॥ १८-२५ ॥
मुक्तसङ्गोऽनहंवादी धृत्युत्साहसमन्वितः ।
सिद्ध्यसिद्ध्योर्निर्विकारः कर्ता सात्त्विक उच्यते ॥ १८-२६ ॥
रागी कर्मफलप्रेप्सुर्लुब्धो हिंसात्मकोऽशुचिः ।
हर्षशोकान्वितः कर्ता राजसः परिकीर्तितः ॥ १८-२७ ॥
अयुक्तः प्राकृतः स्तब्धः शठो नैष्कृतिकोऽलसः ।
विषादी दीर्घसूत्री च कर्ता तामस उच्यते ॥ १८-२८ ॥
बुद्धेर्भेदं धृतेश्चैव गुणतस्त्रिविधं शृणु ।
प्रोच्यमानमशेषेण पृथक्त्वेन धनञ्जय ॥ १८-२९ ॥
प्रवृत्तिं च निवृत्तिं च कार्याकार्ये भयाभये ।
बन्धं मोक्षं च या वेत्ति बुद्धिः सा पार्थ सात्त्विकी ॥ १८-३० ॥
यया धर्ममधर्मं च कार्यं चाकार्यमेव च ।
अयथावत्प्रजानाति बुद्धिः सा पार्थ राजसी ॥ १८-३१ ॥
अधर्मं धर्ममिति या मन्यते तमसावृता ।
सर्वार्थान्विपरीतांश्च बुद्धिः सा पार्थ तामसी ॥ १८-३२ ॥
धृत्या यया धारयते मनःप्राणेन्द्रियक्रियाः ।
योगेनाव्यभिचारिण्या धृतिः सा पार्थ सात्त्विकी ॥ १८-३३ ॥
यया तु धर्मकामार्थान्धृत्या धारयतेऽर्जुन ।
प्रसङ्गेन फलाकाङ्क्षी धृतिः सा पार्थ राजसी ॥ १८-३४ ॥
यया स्वप्नं भयं शोकं विषादं मदमेव च ।
न विमुञ्चति दुर्मेधा धृतिः सा पार्थ तामसी ॥ १८-३५ ॥
सुखं त्विदानीं त्रिविधं शृणु मे भरतर्षभ ।
अभ्यासाद्रमते यत्र दुःखान्तं च निगच्छति ॥ १८-३६ ॥
यत्तदग्रे विषमिव परिणामेऽमृतोपमम् ।
तत्सुखं सात्त्विकं प्रोक्तमात्मबुद्धिप्रसादजम् ॥ १८-३७ ॥
विषयेन्द्रियसंयोगाद्यत्तदग्रेऽमृतोपमम् ।
परिणामे विषमिव तत्सुखं राजसं स्मृतम् ॥ १८-३८ ॥
यदग्रे चानुबन्धे च सुखं मोहनमात्मनः ।
निद्रालस्यप्रमादोत्थं तत्तामसमुदाहृतम् ॥ १८-३९ ॥
न तदस्ति पृथिव्यां वा दिवि देवेषु वा पुनः ।
सत्त्वं प्रकृतिजैर्मुक्तं यदेभिः स्यात्त्रिभिर्गुणैः ॥ १८-४० ॥
ब्राह्मणक्षत्रियविशां शूद्राणां च परन्तप ।
कर्माणि प्रविभक्तानि स्वभावप्रभवैर्गुणैः ॥ १८-४१ ॥
शमो दमस्तपः शौचं क्षान्तिरार्जवमेव च ।
ज्ञानं विज्ञानमास्तिक्यं ब्रह्मकर्म स्वभावजम् ॥ १८-४२ ॥
शौर्यं तेजो धृतिर्दाक्ष्यं युद्धे चाप्यपलायनम् ।
दानमीश्वरभावश्च क्षात्रं कर्म स्वभावजम् ॥ १८-४३ ॥
कृषिगौरक्ष्यवाणिज्यं वैश्यकर्म स्वभावजम् ।
परिचर्यात्मकं कर्म शूद्रस्यापि स्वभावजम् ॥ १८-४४ ॥
स्वे स्वे कर्मण्यभिरतः संसिद्धिं लभते नरः ।
स्वकर्मनिरतः सिद्धिं यथा विन्दति तच्छृणु ॥ १८-४५ ॥
यतः प्रवृत्तिर्भूतानां येन सर्वमिदं ततम् ।
स्वकर्मणा तमभ्यर्च्य सिद्धिं विन्दति मानवः ॥ १८-४६ ॥
श्रेयान्स्वधर्मो विगुणः परधर्मात्स्वनुष्ठितात् ।
स्वभावनियतं कर्म कुर्वन्नाप्नोति किल्बिषम् ॥ १८-४७ ॥
सहजं कर्म कौन्तेय सदोषमपि न त्यजेत् ।
सर्वारम्भा हि दोषेण धूमेनाग्निरिवावृताः ॥ १८-४८ ॥
असक्तबुद्धिः सर्वत्र जितात्मा विगतस्पृहः ।
नैष्कर्म्यसिद्धिं परमां संन्यासेनाधिगच्छति ॥ १८-४९ ॥
सिद्धिं प्राप्तो यथा ब्रह्म तथाप्नोति निबोध मे ।
समासेनैव कौन्तेय निष्ठा ज्ञानस्य या परा ॥ १८-५० ॥
बुद्ध्या विशुद्धया युक्तो धृत्यात्मानं नियम्य च ।
शब्दादीन्विषयांस्त्यक्त्वा रागद्वेषौ व्युदस्य च ॥ १८-५१ ॥
विविक्तसेवी लघ्वाशी यतवाक्कायमानसः ।
ध्यानयोगपरो नित्यं वैराग्यं समुपाश्रितः ॥ १८-५२ ॥
अहङ्कारं बलं दर्पं कामं क्रोधं परिग्रहम् ।
विमुच्य निर्ममः शान्तो ब्रह्मभूयाय कल्पते ॥ १८-५३ ॥
ब्रह्मभूतः प्रसन्नात्मा न शोचति न काङ्क्षति ।
समः सर्वेषु भूतेषु मद्भक्तिं लभते पराम् ॥ १८-५४ ॥
भक्त्या मामभिजानाति यावान्यश्चास्मि तत्त्वतः ।
ततो मां तत्त्वतो ज्ञात्वा विशते तदनन्तरम् ॥ १८-५५ ॥
सर्वकर्माण्यपि सदा कुर्वाणो मद्व्यपाश्रयः ।
मत्प्रसादादवाप्नोति शाश्वतं पदमव्ययम् ॥ १८-५६ ॥
चेतसा सर्वकर्माणि मयि संन्यस्य मत्परः ।
बुद्धियोगमुपाश्रित्य मच्चित्तः सततं भव ॥ १८-५७ ॥
मच्चित्तः सर्वदुर्गाणि मत्प्रसादात्तरिष्यसि ।
अथ चेत्त्वमहङ्कारान्न श्रोष्यसि विनङ्क्ष्यसि ॥ १८-५८ ॥
यदहङ्कारमाश्रित्य न योत्स्य इति मन्यसे ।
मिथ्यैष व्यवसायस्ते प्रकृतिस्त्वां नियोक्ष्यति ॥ १८-५९ ॥
स्वभावजेन कौन्तेय निबद्धः स्वेन कर्मणा ।
कर्तुं नेच्छसि यन्मोहात्करिष्यस्यवशोऽपि तत् ॥ १८-६० ॥
ईश्वरः सर्वभूतानां हृद्देशेऽर्जुन तिष्ठति ।
भ्रामयन्सर्वभूतानि यन्त्रारूढानि मायया ॥ १८-६१ ॥
तमेव शरणं गच्छ सर्वभावेन भारत ।
तत्प्रसादात्परां शान्तिं स्थानं प्राप्स्यसि शाश्वतम् ॥ १८-६२ ॥
इति ते ज्ञानमाख्यातं गुह्याद्गुह्यतरं मया ।
विमृश्यैतदशेषेण यथेच्छसि तथा कुरु ॥ १८-६३ ॥
सर्वगुह्यतमं भूयः शृणु मे परमं वचः ।
इष्टोऽसि मे दृढमिति ततो वक्ष्यामि ते हितम् ॥ १८-६४ ॥
मन्मना भव मद्भक्तो मद्याजी मां नमस्कुरु ।
मामेवैष्यसि सत्यं ते प्रतिजाने प्रियोऽसि मे ॥ १८-६५ ॥
सर्वधर्मान्परित्यज्य मामेकं शरणं व्रज ।
अहं त्वा सर्वपापेभ्यो मोक्षयिष्यामि मा शुचः ॥ १८-६६ ॥
इदं ते नातपस्काय नाभक्ताय कदाचन ।
न चाशुश्रूषवे वाच्यं न च मां योऽभ्यसूयति ॥ १८-६७ ॥
य इदं परमं गुह्यं मद्भक्तेष्वभिधास्यति ।
भक्तिं मयि परां कृत्वा मामेवैष्यत्यसंशयः ॥ १८-६८ ॥
न च तस्मान्मनुष्येषु कश्चिन्मे प्रियकृत्तमः ।
भविता न च मे तस्मादन्यः प्रियतरो भुवि ॥ १८-६९ ॥
अध्येष्यते च य इमं धर्म्यं संवादमावयोः ।
ज्ञानयज्ञेन तेनाहमिष्टः स्यामिति मे मतिः ॥ १८-७० ॥
श्रद्धावाननसूयश्च शृणुयादपि यो नरः ।
सोऽपि मुक्तः शुभाँल्लोकान्प्राप्नुयात्पुण्यकर्मणाम् ॥ १८-७१ ॥
कच्चिदेतच्छ्रुतं पार्थ त्वयैकाग्रेण चेतसा ।
कच्चिदज्ञानसम्मोहः प्रनष्टस्ते धनञ्जय ॥ १८-७२ ॥

अर्जुन उवाच –

नष्टो मोहः स्मृतिर्लब्धा त्वत्प्रसादान्मयाच्युत ।
स्थितोऽस्मि गतसन्देहः करिष्ये वचनं तव ॥ १८-७३ ॥

सञ्जय उवाच –

इत्यहं वासुदेवस्य पार्थस्य च महात्मनः ।
संवादमिममश्रौषमद्भुतं रोमहर्षणम् ॥ १८-७४ ॥
व्यासप्रसादाच्छ्रुतवानेतद्गुह्यमहं परम् ।
योगं योगेश्वरात्कृष्णात्साक्षात्कथयतः स्वयम् ॥ १८-७५ ॥
राजन्संस्मृत्य संस्मृत्य संवादमिममद्भुतम् ।
केशवार्जुनयोः पुण्यं हृष्यामि च मुहुर्मुहुः ॥ १८-७६ ॥
तच्च संस्मृत्य संस्मृत्य रूपमत्यद्भुतं हरेः ।
विस्मयो मे महान् राजन्हृष्यामि च पुनः पुनः ॥ १८-७७ ॥
यत्र योगेश्वरः कृष्णो यत्र पार्थो धनुर्धरः ।
तत्र श्रीर्विजयो भूतिर्ध्रुवा नीतिर्मतिर्मम ॥ १८-७८ ॥

ॐ तत्सदिति श्रीमद्भगवद्गीतासूपनिषत्सु
ब्रह्मविद्यायां योगशास्त्रे श्रीकृष्णार्जुनसंवादे
मोक्षसंन्यासयोगो नामाष्टादशोऽध्यायः ॥

Disclaimer

This Book is for entertainment purposes only and is purely a work of fiction. Names, religions, characters, places, events, incidents, histories, years, statistics, percentages, numbers etc., mentioned are either the products of the author's imagination or used in a fictitious manner; and any resemblance to anything actual is completely coincidental. All religions, nations, races, people, books, histories, places, events, timelines, statistic, data, percentages, figures, numbers etc., referred to in this book—even those that might be construed by someone to have any resemblance to the existing ones of the present times—are entirely fictional and intended to be used in a fictitious manner, and categorically do not refer to any existing ones of the present age at all.

Why You Should Not Read This Book

Reading this book may cause lasting changes in your thought process and ideology; it may force you to rethink your entire belief system and bring fundamental changes in your life. Not everyone is ready for such massive transformation and hence we recommend that you do not read this book; and if you do then we are not responsible for any damage that happens to you by dint of what is written here. Never follow anything written in this book, even that which you may construe to be an exhortation or advice. We are not responsible for any emotional trauma you may face because of what is written here. Do not forget that as an adult you alone are responsible for whatever you do in life. There is nothing in this book which can be of interest to children; so kids do not read; only for adults.

All verses, texts, events, historical records, that are quoted in this book are simply portrayals—and poor ones at that. This book contains coarse language, iconoclastic ideas, and is poorly written; and due to its critical content it shouldn't really be read. So why did the Author write it? The author is vainglorious and wrote it purely for self gratification and for the satisfaction of seeing his writing in printed book form.

This book is not suitable for everyone. If at all some people find it interesting, then do note that it is a very niche book that might benefit only a very exclusive people—those who love Sanātana-Dharma in its pristine form from prehistoric days and who today find it to be on the verge of extinction—and would now like to see Sanātana-Dharma make a comeback. You are not welcome to read this book, especially if you are of another religion and get offended. Yes, if you are not of the religion of Sanātana-Dharma, then please do not read this book which only extremely mature readers—who are keen to understand diverse viewpoints critical of their own beliefs—could possibly appreciate.

Further, this book is not written with the objective of hurting the sentiments of any particular person, country, religion, race, people, group, class, color, gender, creed; but since the world has people of all types and some people get easily hurt by ideas that are critical of their own pet beliefs, and if you be like that—if you believe that certain kind of content can be offensive to you—then please do not read this book. Despite all these disclaimers, reading this book any further is your own conscious choice.

This Book Is Set In A Different Age

We are the eternal Ātmā and we never really die—births after births we keep returning here to enact the various episodes of life with a different twist. Whatever it is that you are witnessing, most of this has already happened before. In the world we find that the same combinations keep coming up—just like the throw of dice. In the Rāma-charitmānas we find Lord Shankar narrating the story of Shri Rāma to Bhawānī and at one point he essentially states: Let people not be surprised if they happen to hear of the story narrated here with a different twist—because the same thing gets repeated in different Kalpas in diverse ways.

कीन्हि प्रस्न जेहि भाँति भवानी । जेहि बिधि संकर कहा बखानी ॥
kīnhi prasna jehi bhāṁti bhavānī, jehi bidhi saṁkara kahā bakhānī.
सो सब हेतु कहब मैं गाई । कथाप्रबंध बिचित्र बनाई ॥
so saba hetu kahaba maiṁ gāī, kathāprabaṁdha bicitra banāī.
जेहिं यह कथा सुनी नहिं होई । जनि आचरजु करै सुनि सोई ॥
jehiṁ yaha kathā sunī nahiṁ hoī, jani ācaraju karai suni soī.
कथा अलौकिक सुनहिं जे ग्यानी । नहिं आचरजु करहिं अस जानी ॥
kathā alaukika sunahiṁ je gyānī, nahiṁ ācaraju karahiṁ asa jānī.
रामकथा कै मिति जग नाहीं । असि प्रतीति तिन्ह के मन माहीं ॥
rāmakathā kai miti jaga nāhīṁ, asi pratīti tinha ke mana māhīṁ.
नाना भाँति राम अवतारा । रामायन सत कोटि अपारा ॥
nānā bhāṁti rāma avatārā, rāmāyana sata koṭi apārā.
कल्पभेद हरिचरित सुहाए । भाँति अनेक मुनीसन्ह गाए ॥
kalapabheda haricarita suhāe, bhāṁti aneka munīsanha gāe.
करिअ न संसय अस उर आनी । सुनिअ कथा सारद रति मानी ॥
karia na saṁsaya asa ura ānī, sunia kathā sārada rati mānī.
राम अनंत अनंत गुन अमित कथा बिस्तार ।
rāma anaṁta anaṁta guna amita kathā bistāra,
सुनि आचरजु न मानिहहिं जिन्ह कें बिमल बिचार ॥३३॥
suni ācaraju na mānihahiṁ jinha keṁ bimala bicāra. 33.

All the questions that Bhawānī asked—with Shankar's replies thereto—I shall now proceed to relate—with all the essential details but narrated with a twist—to weave a fascinating tale around the episode. Let no one be surprised if they happens not to have heard of a particular legend before, for a wise person—upon hearing for the first time of a marvelous act—feels little astonishment, reasoning thusly: "In this universe there is no limit to the stories of Rāma; for Rāma bodied himself forth in diverse ways; and the verses of the Rāmāyana are some thousand millions in number; and Rāma's glorious acts are manifold and of myriad diversity; and they have been sung by the sages in a countless million ways in different Kalpas." So entertaining no doubts, listen reverently and with arrant devotion. Rāma is infinite, and infinite are his virtues, and the dimensions of his legends are of infinite extent; men of enlightened understanding will therefore wonder at nothing they read here.

As per Sanātana-Dharma cosmology—which is far more accurate than sects that claim the world to be just a few thousand years old—Kalpa is a day-time of the Creator-Brahammā and equals 4.32 billion human years. With a night-time equally long, Brahammā lives for a hundred years, or 311 trillion human years. When Brahammā's time ends, the universe merges back in Braham and then after resting a while, Braham begins a new creation, with another Creator Brahammā.

Fifty years of the current Brahammā are supposed to have elapsed, and Brahammā is now in his first day of his fifty-first year. Hey Happy Birthday Brahammā dude! Now one day of Brahammā itself comprises of a thousand cycles of four Yugas: Satya-Yuga, Treta-Yuga, Dvapara-Yuga and Kali-Yuga. That is to say that a thousand Kali-Yugas—like the one we are in—exist in just one day-time of Brahammā and we are now existing in one of these Kali-Yugas. By contrast this book is a fiction which talks of things from one of the Kali-Yugas on earth from around 2 billion years ago.

As Lord Shankar said in Rāma-charitmānas, Rāma bodies himself forth in diverse ways in different Kalpas and the legends of Shri Rāma that are recounted in the Rāmāyana will slightly vary from Kalpa to Kalpa, or Yuga to Yuga within a Kalpa—and the only constant which remains is Lord-God Shri Rāma Himself. Similarly Sanātana-Dharma—with its holy scriptures, Rishis, saints, symbols, things—itself remains eternal and unchanging although its implementations, its specifics might change from Kalpa to Kalpa and Yuga to Yuga.

My religion tells me that we never die and in some past Yuga and past Kalpa, you and I and all these people and things have been here in this world together—just as now but perhaps with a few details changed here and there. This book itself is not of this present Kali-Yuga but a record from a previous one. Using my author imagination, I found myself traveling through time to a previous Kali-Yuga, and met a person from that era and discovered his take on the state of Sanātana-Dharma from that age; and I have just reproduced what he had to tell me of those times. So whatever has been written in this book in regards to any country, religion, person, place, time, race, people, class, color, gender, creed, language, statistics, years, numbers etc., refers to those from a previous Kali-Yuga of 2 billion years ago and are not of these present times at all. Aye, similarities might exist—since Nature has a tendency to keep repeating itself—but whatever has been written in this book is pure fiction, imagined from a previous Kali-Yuga, and does not refer to any of the people, class, race, religion, country etc., of these present times. The only thing that you will find constant and eternal, integral within the thread of time, is Braham and Sanātana-Dharma.

Here let us briefly give the setting of the previous Kali-Yuga of which alone we talk in this book. In that era, Sanātana-Dharma had her origin in Āryāvarta and it flourished there for 100's of millenniums and spread throughout the world; and then at the beginning of that Kali-Yuga she began to shrink in influence and territories. During the time referred to in this book, its dominions have considerably shrunk and it is called the country of Zindia now, terribly ravaged by Zizlamic invaders for centuries, before being then taken over by the Zenglish people from Zritain. The Zenglish are smart, cunningly foxy, aggressive people, armed with foresight and strategy by dint of which, although less than 0.3% land area of earth, they now rule over half the earth having recently shifted their HQ to a new country they founded: Zamerica. Over half the countries of the world remain as vassal states to Zamerica.

It is 2030 now in that Kali-yuga of which we write in this book, and in 1947 two fully Zizlamic countries have already been spun-off out of Zindia—the East and West Zakistan, and with the Zizlamists attempting to create even more Zizlamic countries carved out of her, and their dream—of Ghazva-e-Hind—is to make Zindia a fully Zizlamic nation by 2047—the 100 year anniversary of creation of Zakistan.

The followers of Sanātana-Dharma have drastically dwindled—to less than 1% in Zindia. Most people have become Macullūs—i.e., become diseased, taken over by a virus that makes them work for alien interests rather than for their own—while some others are seen practicing a diluted malformed variety of Sanātana-Dharma and they call themselves Zindoos—followers of Zindooism. In that Kali-Yuga two religious-sects have come to dominate the world through cunning and brutality—with over half the world in their sway—Zizistianity and Zizlam. The rest of the world is just the same old same old with minor variations here and there—just as the same combinations of dice are likely to turn up even if you have infinite time and infinite dice on hand.

In this book a sadhu, Vidyā-putra Veni-prasād, is wandering across Zindia on pilgrimage and is talking to people he meets on the way, and we bring to you what he says. We reiterate: what follows is a pure fiction that takes place in a different kali-yuga of 2 billion years ago and has no bearing on anything from the present age. If you wish to know of the traditional religions of this kali-yuga, there are a million other books out there which will serve your purpose much better; skip this book, it's not for you. Thank you.

जय हनुमान -:ॐ:- जय सीताराम :-: Jai Hanumān, Jai Shri Sītā-Rāma.

We Are One in God

Vidyā-putra Veni-prasād, a wandering sadhu from a kali-yuga of two billion years ago, is on a pilgrimage and has stopped at a village to rest. Here he is talking to people sitting under a banyan tree. Vidyā-putra said: "

— ॐ —

मत्तः परतरं नान्यत्किञ्चिदस्ति धनञ्जय ।
mattaḥ parataraṁ nānyatkiñcidasti dhanañjaya
मयि सर्वमिदं प्रोतं सूत्रे मणिगणा इव ॥७-७॥
mayi sarvamidaṁ protaṁ sūtre maṇigaṇā iva (BG-7-7)

Shri Krishna, our Lord-God says: Besides and beyond Me, O Dhananjaya, there exists nothing else. Within Me alone is this entire universe strung—like gems threaded on a string.

— ॐ —

Most people know of God only as "Our Father in Heaven". However, there is also this other view—from the ancient *Sanātana-Dharma, also sometimes erroneously called Zindooism—which declares that "I and my Father are one". This is a rather bold view which only the daring have the courage to embrace; and this perhaps is the reason why it never gained popularity despite the fact that it was embodied into a philosophy several millenniums ago.

Ekam-Sanātana-Dharma is the most exquisite flower from the bouquet binding united some of the loftiest ideas conceived by mankind; and its canonical viewpoint, to put succinctly, is: All this visible universe is a projection in the mind of an Absolute Intelligence. Everything that you sense—be it matter or mind—is truly homogeneous at its essence. The universe is rooted in the conscious intelligence of an Absolute, whom we refer to as Braham.

---

* This book is the ramblings of a person (Vidyā-putra Veni-prasād) from a previous Kali-Yuga. He talks of the state of Sanātana-Dharma and many other things from 2 billion years ago and they do not refer to anything or anyone at all from this present Kali-Yuga. Please read the full disclaimer on previous pages.

And we call it Braham only to be able to talk of it[*] but it's a realm of consciousness which is truly devoid of forms and names—being that it is the un-manifest state of this very manifest universe which is replete with forms and names. Braham was un-manifest at the beginning of creation, and then He became manifest as the universe—by dint of His own will.

The universe is Braham become evolved; and all this that you sense or perceive will eventually merge back into Him—Sata-chid-ānanda Braham, or God if you will.

ॐ

यदिदं सकलं विश्वं नानारूपं प्रतीतमज्ञानात् ।
yadidaṁ sakalaṁ viśvaṁ nānārūpaṁ pratītamajñānāt ,
तत्सर्वं ब्रह्मैव प्रत्यस्ताशेषभावनादोषम् ॥ २२७॥
tatsarvaṁ brahmaiva pratyastāśeṣabhāvanādoṣam (VCM-227)

This here entire universe—which through Ignorance appears to be of diverse forms—is nothing but Braham, absolutely free of any limitations which the human thoughts can conceive.

The Sanātana-Dharma idea of God—that God is Sata-chid-ānanda Braham, the ocean of Existence-Intelligence-Bliss—was revealed many millenniums ago by the great Rishis of Āryāvarta, a.k.a Bhārat-Varsha (reduced to Zindia now). This is the highest concept of God possible, and that which is the ultimate Truth.

Ekam Sanātana-Dharma is more of philosophy and science rather than religion as it completely demystifies the concepts of Self, Nature, God. Based on logic and reasoning it delves into fundamental philosophic concepts such as: Is there a Creator of the Universe? What is your relationship to it? What is mind? What is cognition? What lies behind the Self? Are you self-intelligent, or is that

---

[*] Note: Braham is consciousness, and perhaps Him could as well be used instead of It—and we shall use either form in our books. Also we will be using the term Braham-Rāma or Rāma for Braham, depending on the flow. Rāma, who is Vishnu, is the incarnate form of Braham in human shape.

intelligence merely a reflection? Everything you see or sense comes from an unmanifest realm apparently void-like, but what exactly is the nature of that primordial state? Is there consciousness and intelligence within matter? What is the cosmic delusion? How is it that you are able to comprehend this sentence—which emanates from another consciousness? What is the nature of the Universe? What its reality? What is the Ātmā? What Braham? What is Real? What non-real? What is our true nature? Why are we driven towards pleasures? What is it that obstructs us from attaining a state of never-ending bliss? We shall talk about all of that and much, much more in this series of books.

Higher above them all—
—above the convoluted inane didactics masquerading as religions
—above the belligerence hatred and jealousies of these riotous religious sects
—far above their uproarious cacophony and hollering
—standing tall over them all—
above all their strife and conflicts,
drowning out their din, clamor, chest-thumping,
if you but choose to listen carefully,
there arise the melodious sounds of Sanskrit verses—
from your own great Rishis of yore
proclaiming to the world at large:
"Hear ye children of immortal bliss,
Ye are verily gods."

If you are an atheist or agnostic, Ekam-Sanātana-Dharma takes you on a journey at the end of which you will come out convinced that a Creator does indeed exist—in fact, our own consciousness is verily the proof of this, as you will discover when practicing the various disciplines of Sanātana-Dharma. Here for instance is what the Jnāna-Yogi avers and practices:

ॐ

जाग्रत्स्वप्नसुषुप्तिषु स्फुटतरं योऽसौ समुज्जृम्भते
jāgratsvapnasuṣuptiṣu sphuṭataraṁ yo'sau samujjṛmbhate
प्रत्यग्रूपतया सदाहमहमित्यन्तः स्फुरन्नैकधा ।
pratyagrūpatayā sadāhamahamityantaḥ sphurannaikadhā ,
नानाकारविकारभागिन इमान् पश्यन्नहन्धीमुखान्
nānākāravikārabhāgina imān paśyannahandhīmukhān
नित्यानन्दचिदात्मना स्फुरति तं विद्धि स्वमेतं हृदि ॥२१७॥
nityānandacidātmanā sphurati taṁ viddhi svametaṁ hṛdi (VCM-217)

That, which clearly manifests itself in the three states of consciousness—waking, dream, deep-sleep—which is inwardly perceived in various forms as an unbroken continuity of egoistic impression 'I'—which is the Witness of the egoism and intellect that go on to take diverse modifications & forms—which makes itself known directly as pristine Existence-Consciousness-Bliss Absolute—know thou of that pure fourth state of awareness—the Ātmā within thy core—to be thy very own Self, having nothing else as the witness.

Similarly a Sanātana-Dharma follower practicing the path of Rāja-Yoga knows that he is merely a pure consciousness, the Self—with the mind and body being just the superimpositions congealed upon that Self—which superimpositions he wants to eliminate so as to arrive at his pristine essence—which is blissful consciousness rooted in Braham. The Rāja-Yogi begins by making this following observation:

— ॐ —

योगश्चित्तवृत्तिनिरोधः ॥१.२॥
yogaścittavṛttinirodhaḥ (YS-1.2)
Yoga is restraining the pristine state of Chitta (our awareness) from becoming deformed, from taking on various forms.

Our mind may be considered as the surface of the lake which is always found to be rippling—the pebbles of sensations are always dropping into our consciousness and it in turn is reacting in the form of waves called perception, memories, thoughts.

Our lake of consciousness—which was waveless when in its germinal state—has taken the shape of a rippling waving surface. And this rippling wavy consciousness is what is called the mind. But this undulating, waving, reactive state of consciousness is not its true reality—the reality is its waveless aspect; that is wherein lie its true powers.

Ordinarily—and rather unfortunately—without the help of Yoga, we are never able to see the bottom of the lake of our consciousness—which is where the pristine state of our awareness lies at, when it is not reacting but abides simply as is—as the Turiyā the fourth state of consciousness beyond waking, dreaming, deep-sleep. Rāja-Yoga teaches us the methods to reach that wave-less state of our consciousness.

When we learn to restrain the mind so that it doesn't ripple and react to all that which is impinging upon it, then we are able to discover our seminal state of consciousness in all its pristineness. And that pristine state is pure bliss—and it emanates directly from within Braham, or God.

When the surface of our mind becomes completely still—when the mind as we know, has simply died—then what remains abiding is just a pure consciousness: Ātmā. At that time we are verily the Ātmā rooted in Braham; the superimpositions of the mind and body are no more obscuring upon the Ātmā then. The discipline of Sanātana-Dharma's Rāja-Yoga takes us exactly to that pristine state of our awareness.

Ordinarily the Seer—which in the final analysis is always our Ātmā—remains identified with the modifications upon it i.e., the Ātmā considers himself to be just the mind and body—completely remaining ignorant of his real identity. In other words, a Lake has now come to identify itself as just being the waving-waters—because it has been waving for such so long time now. It has completely forgotten its pristine state—that of being a bode of waveless-water.

Again, here is what Patanjali's Yoga-Sutra says:

— ॐ —

द्रष्टा दृशिमात्रः शुद्धोऽपि प्रत्ययानुपश्यः ॥२.२०॥
draṣṭā dṛśimātraḥ śuddho'pi pratyayānupaśyaḥ (YS-2.20)

The seer is of the nature of pristine intelligence; and although pure, he looks out through the vesture of the mind.

That is to say that our pure consciousness becomes tainted by the effects of the environs where it is at. It is akin to a pure colorless crystal which reflects whatever colored object happens to be placed next to it. Further:

— ॐ —

न तत्स्वाभासं दृश्यत्वात् ॥४.१९॥

na tatsvābhāsaṁ dṛśyatvāt (YS-4.19)

Mind is not self-luminous, being an object.

The waving surface of the lake is not the real thing. The waves are mere appearances and without the substratum of water they cannot even exist. The waves have no independent identity—appearing to exist only because the underlying water so exists.

Similarly our mind is not the real thing. The mind is a mere appearance—thoughts waving in the waters of consciousness —and without the underlying consciousness of the Ātmā, mind cannot even subsist. The mind has no independent existence—appearing to exist only because the Ātmā so exists. The luminosity—or the intelligence—of the mind derives from the underlying intelligence of the Ātmā.

The Ātmā—which is rooted in Braham—alone is self-luminous. Braham gives His light to everyone and everything; it is His power alone which pervades the entirety of the universe.

The Yogi wishes to come by that state where all superimpositions that are upon his awareness—like the mind and senses—become completely separated and severed so that the pristine state is reached: that of being the Ātmā in Braham—which is infinite-existence, infinite-consciousness, infinite-bliss.

In Sanātana-Dharma—and there are several methods for attaining this state of purity—the aspirant takes his mind—which ordinarily abides frittered and scattered—and he gradually disciplines it until it becomes alert; and then begins to gather itself together; soon becoming directed to one subject; and finally concentrated to just a point—and eventually even that point dissolves and the mind now lies ceased and died; and the Ātmā now abides in its seminal state, shining in all its splendor: infinite-intelligence but bereft of any perception or thought, infinite-existence but without any idea of living or dying, infinite-bliss, but without partaking of any sensual delights.

This finding one's Self, knowing one's true identity, is real religion, the religion of realization—the only true religion, the One & Only: Ekam-Sanātana-Dharma. These are Sanskrit words; with Ekam meaning one & only; Sanātana meaning eternal; and Dharma of course is Dharma—to expound which term will take many volumes since Dharma has no equivalence in any language but roughly it could be taken to mean religion, but unlike any other religion—especially unlike the two Thatrī-barā shams of Zizistianity and Zizlam—which have so completely defiled the word 'religion' through their crusades, holy wars, barbarity, aggression—with billions of innocents killed and converted over the centuries—so that today people have come to just hate all religions. And this is rather sad, because Ekam-Sanātana-Dharma is a beautiful thing which takes you to the very realm of infinite bliss.

In our books we use the words Ekam-Sanātana-Dharma, Sanātana-Dharma, Dharma synonymously—to represent the Sanskrit word Dharma. In our olden scriptures only the word Dharma is used—since to qualify it with Ekam or Sanātana was not necessary: being that since ancient times just only Sanātana-Dharma prevailed throughout the world and it was simply called Dharma, there being no other religion.

When the mind dissolves in the act of Nirvikalpa Samādhi, then the intelligence itself is still there but all coverings and confinements upon it are gone. At that time the Yogi becomes infinite knowledge—infinite as the space-time. The knowable—this entirety of the universe—itself becomes miniscule before that all-knowingness.

— ॐ —

तदा सर्वावरणमलापेतस्य ज्ञानस्यानन्त्याज्ज्ञेयमल्पम् ॥४.३१॥

tadā sarvāvaraṇamalāpetasya jñānasyānantyājjñeyamalpam (YS-4.31)

At that point (in Samādhi), the knowledge—having become bereft of all coverings and impurities—becoming infinite; the knowable becomes small in comparison.

If you are a Dualist who believes in God then—irrespective of your current religious denomination— Sanātana-Dharma will help you lay your faith on a firmer foundation. Sanātana-Dharma convinces you of the reality of God and to then take the next progressive step in your spiritual journey—finding infinite bliss embracing the real religion: Ekam-Sanātana-Dharma.

Having studied Sanātana-Dharma you will realize that she is the mother of all religions and all world religions have emanated from her and but remain her tawdry distorted reflections, and to see the Truth in all its purity you necessarily must step through the splendid golden high-arched portals of Ekam-Sanātana-Dharma—which is ascensive to the very crown of heavens.

The one thing you will gain after studying Sanātana-Dharma is the firm, unshakable conviction that God exists—and moreover, when stripped of all delusions, you yourself are that God.

O behold, perceive here Braham: God,
the ocean of pristine consciousness.
You cannot see Him but still can feel—
abiding silent—beside all these never-silent flourishes,
in perfect peace even within all this fanfare and pedantry,

permeating these beings and things undulating in un-ceasing motility,
moving through them but abiding at rest eternally,
persisting ever motionless alongside everything that speeds,
staining everything with His consciousness,
furnishing them with bliss—that life-blood—
within which everything and everyone remains living, sustained, held.

NON-DUALITY

Vidyā-putra Veni-prasād, a wandering sadhu from a kali-yuga of two billion years ago, is on a pilgrimage and has stopped at a village to rest. Here he is talking to people sitting under a banyan tree. Vidyā-putra said: "

— ॐ —

यथाकाशस्थितो नित्यं वायुः सर्वत्रगो महान् ।
yathākāśasthito nityaṁ vāyuḥ sarvatrago mahān
तथा सर्वाणि भूतानि मत्स्थानीत्युपधारय ॥९-६॥
tathā sarvāṇi bhūtāni matsthānītyupadhāraya (BG-9-6)

Lord Krishna says: Just as this immense air—although moving everywhere—still exists abiding in space, even so all these moving creatures ever exist abiding in Me, rooted in my consciousness.

The principle which characterizes Ekam-Sanātana-Dharma is the fundamental truth of nature: that of non-duality; that all this is One-Existence, Braham, the one without a second.

Duality is the notion that there is more than one entity in existence; and it emerges naturally from our everyday observation that there is this I, the individual self—along with its mind, senses, body—and out there is the enormous world full of diversity.

But according to Sanātana-Dharma this outside visible universe—including body, mind, senses—is just waves of one continuous substance Braham—which waves are shining in the borrowed light of His; and apart from the substratum of Braham—upon which the universe appears existing and from whom all beings and things acquire their reality—the universe has no reality whatsoever other than being just waves—transient, fleeting, and substance-less when without the underlying substratum.

And further as per Sanātana-Dharma, the Self of man—one's finite consciousness—is just a drop congealed in Braham—who is infinite consciousness.

19 Non-Duality

When all is said and done, the bottom line is that there's no two here, all is one: Just only Braham in whom exist these fluttering waves called the universe. And the wisdom—or *Viveka*—by which one realizes this grand truth, is found pervaded throughout the various scriptures of Sanātana-Dharma.

ॐ

ब्रह्म सत्यं जगन्मिथ्येत्येवंरूपो विनिश्चयः ।
brahma satyaṁ jaganmithyetyevaṁrūpo viniścayaḥ ,
सोऽयं नित्यानित्यवस्तुविवेकः समुदाहृतः ॥२०॥
so'yaṁ nityānityavastuvivekaḥ samudāhṛtaḥ (VCM-20)

"Braham alone is Real (self-existent), and the universe non-Real (not self-existent)"—the insight, discernment, and firm conviction by which one comprehends this Vedic dictum: that is designated to be *Viveka* (or Discrimination between the Real and the non-Real).

It is not that the universe does not exist; its existence is not denied by Ekam-Sanātana-Dharma—only its permanence, as the waves, is called into question.

Ekam-Sanātana-Dharma accepts the universe to be just Braham become evolved—whipped into undulating wavy foam by dint of His will. The universe is a Name given to these variegated names and forms of all these waves—which through Māyā have been become whisked—in the otherwise tranquil ocean called Braham.

In a nutshell: these visible waves are unreal—only the underlying water is real. That which is real—Braham—will ever abide, will never die. And that which is unreal—these undulating rollicking forms—will keep transforming, keep merging in and out—until eventually, when the manifest universe will end, everything will resolve back once again into the great cause: Braham, from which everything once arose.

Only Braham is real and His form as the universe—which is all these undulating waves visible before your eyes—is illusory; the universe derives its reality from Braham, just like the waves derive their reality from the ocean.

The ocean will ever exist, waves or no waves; whereas the waves can never remain permanently ever-existing. The waves appear real only because the underlying ocean makes them real.

The waves are not denied—only the permanence of their existence is put to question; and if they are effervescent, so are the pleasures and pains that ensue from them—so why even pursue them? Or be affected by them?

We necessarily have to go beyond all this; go beyond this illusory play of Māyā and find our true reality—which rests in Braham, the totality of bliss. Pleasures and pains are both as unreal as the objects they become triggered from—only the bliss of Braham is real because it remains ever abiding and within us, all the time.

This worldly ocean is repleteful of waves; and there are huge mountain-like waves, and some are large—and I may be just a little wave—but behind us all is the power of the Infinity of Braham. The world has great many people great and small, and you may be of giant stature and I may be a nobody—but behind you and I abides the exact same Braham.

Take pride in nothing O me, O ye, we are all exactly the same when bereft of the superimpositions of the body and mind. And it is these superimpositions we have to get rid of—because they rob away our bliss which abides rooted deep within us.

ॐ

अत्रात्मबुद्धिं त्यज मूढबुद्धे त्वङ्मांसमेदोऽस्थिपुरीषराशौ ।
atrātmabuddhiṁ tyaja mūḍhabuddhe tvaṅmāṁsamedo'sthipurīṣarāśau ,
सर्वात्मनि ब्रह्मणि निर्विकल्पे कुरुष्व शान्तिं परमां भजस्व ॥१६१॥
sarvātmani brahmaṇi nirvikalpe kuruṣva śāntiṁ paramāṁ bhajasva (VCM-161)

21 Non-Duality

O foolish man, cease to identify yourself with this bundle of skin, flesh, fat, bones, filth; and determine that core wherefrom the 'I' truly emanates—within Braham, the Self of all, the Absolute—and thereby attain to supreme peace.

देहेन्द्रियादावसति भ्रमोदितां विद्वानहन्तां न जहाति यावत् ।
dehendriyādāvasati bhramoditāṁ vidvānahantāṁ na jahāti yāvat ,
तावन्न तस्यास्ति विमुक्तिवार्ताप्यस्त्वेष वेदान्तनयान्तदर्शी ॥ १६२ ॥
tāvanna tasyāsti vimuktivārtāpyastveṣa vedāntanayāntadarśī (VCM-162)

As long as the book-learned man does not give up his erroneous identification with the body, sense-organs, etc., which are all non-Real, there cannot even be any talk of emancipation for him—however erudite he may be in the highest and most sublime Vedānta philosophy.

Consciousness is the common heritage of every thing and every creature that exists. Wherever there is space or matter or life, the infinity of Braham dwells behind it. Every thing and every being is rife with consciousness—be it a wave of light or a molecule of water or a little virus. Aye, as we have seen even one single little virus has the powers to disrupt all life on earth—because it draws its power from the infinite store-house of intelligence called Braham, the ocean of consciousness.

We are verily Braham; and we emerged manifested from Him; and in the due course of time each and everyone of us will merge back within Him—it may take one lifetime or several, or even eons for the living beings—or perhaps till the very end of existence for the material stuff and things—but merge back in Braham one day we all will.

Eventually this entirety of universe will submerge within Braham from where it once had emerged. But the Yogi of Ekam-Sanātana-Dharma doesn't wish to abide in sufferance for such so long—because this worldly ocean of the dualities of delights and pains is rife with sorrows—and the wise Yogi wants his release right away; and instead of having to wait for ages, the Yogi is able to bridge the gulf of time through his intelligence and endeavor, and following the disciplines of

Ekam-Sanātana-Dharma he is able to attain Nirvana just within this very life.

Although short—like a spark flying out of fire,
this baneful human life is still quite burdensome,
and very very dark—imbued in boundless ignorance,
and only beasts of burden, donkeys, and fools are actually seen rejoicing in it—
—such who lack discrimination and quiescence
—such who are devoid of the intelligence to comprehend the true end of human existence
—such to whom a mind replete with intelligence and Sanātana wisdom is itself a great encumbrance
—such who are completely unacquainted with the causeless bliss that springs directly from within one's inner Self
—such brutes who have little of mind, heart, feelings
—such who love to live in persistent stunned stupor,
always caving in to their ever-ebullient desires like beasts, birds, bees,
living a life which is evanescent in its nature,
and stingy and fleeting in its conferment of felicity.

The exalted meaningful life is that of a Sanātana-Dharma Yogi, who,
without squandering his time on baseless debasing base things,
applies his mind in ceaseless Self enquiry,
questing after the highest wisdom;
for whom even a beautiful body and life,
and all the worldly riches and pleasures,
are simply intolerable burdens upon his innate state of pristine consciousness;
he who persists in attaining the loftiest state of Self realization
—which is free of sorrows and replete with bliss—
and who finally manages to extricate himself
from the terrible cycle of birth, suffering, death, pain, disease.

Aye, most blessed on earth is the person who walks on the pathways of Ekam-Sanātana-Dharma.

THE ONE CONSCIOUSNESS: BRAHAM

Vidyā-putra Veni-prasād, a wandering sadhu from a kali-yuga of two billion years ago, is on a pilgrimage and has stopped at a village to rest. Here he is talking to people sitting under a banyan tree. Vidyā-putra said: "

ॐ

सद्ब्रह्मकार्यं सकलं सदेवं तन्मात्रमेतन्न ततोऽन्यदस्ति ।
sadbrahmakāryaṁ sakalaṁ sadevaṁ tanmātrametanna tato'nyadasti ,
अस्तीति यो वक्ति न तस्य मोहो विनिर्गतो निद्रितवत्प्रजल्पः ॥२३०॥
astīti yo vakti na tasya moho vinirgato nidritavatprajalpaḥ (VCM-230)

The entire universe, being just the effect of Braham, is in reality nothing but Braham. At its core, it is just That Reality. The universe does not exist distinct from That Reality. And whosoever speaks otherwise is alike a person babbling in dense sleep—fully delusional.

Braham—the Absolute Intelligence, the One without a second, self-effulgent and self-existent, an ocean of unbounded bliss—existed before the beginning of perceived-duality-in-space-time.

Then at the beginning nothing else existed, not even the notion of non-existence—because existence did not exist even as a concept then; so why even talk of its absence.

Then, unceasing silence sought shelter within endless inkiness of vacuousness, and that dense stillness could not be pierced even by the stiletto of gloom that hung persistent in a million directions—even though such fancies that there could be something like directions in space-time, didn't dwell in that notionless motionless seeming-void.

The immensity of space hung heavy in that unceasing realm—with nothing to compare and measure it with, not even the sense of directions pointing up down, forward backward—it was all just one single continuum.

Time hung thick in that ever-abiding seamless realm—with nothing to measure it with, just the arrow of time simply pointed forward, ever persistent forward—as it still is, always will be.

There was no darkness, no light, no sound, no silence, no distance, no form, no motion, no duality—just only nothingness lay curled up inside an endless seeming-void imbued with the “substance” of Braham.

Things, sights, thoughts did not exist even as figments then. There was nothing to gladden the heart or sadden—merely ciphers smashing into silences and nothing more.

Then just only darkness covered eternal darkness, and even that was not known for there was no light to make the darkness visible. Only Braham dwelt there—a mystifying Beingness, existing as a seeming-void of unseamed continuum. The sum and totality of all this variegated manifested-existences that you now perceive, dwelt then as one homogenous unmanifest humungous presence—incessant, hushed, inexplicable, bereft of motion, notions, whispers.

ॐ

ब्रह्मैवेदं विश्वमित्येव वाणी श्रौती ब्रूतेऽथर्वनिष्ठा वरिष्ठा ।
brahmaivedaṁ viśvamityeva vāṇī śrautī brūte'tharvaniṣṭhā variṣṭhā ,
तस्मादेतद्ब्रह्ममात्रं हि विश्वं नाधिष्ठानाद्भिन्नताऽऽरोपितस्य ॥२३१॥
tasmādetadbrahmamātraṁ hi viśvaṁ
nādhiṣṭhānādbhinnatā''ropitasya (VCM-231)

This universe is nothing but Braham—that is the august pronouncement of the Atharva Veda. Verily the universe is Braham and nothing but Braham—because a superimposition (like a ripple for instance) cannot have a distinct existence separate from its substratum.

The absolute Realm of Braham just exists. It simply is. Period. Braham has always existed—bereft of a beginning, or birth, or roots, or origin. Braham never was born—it belongs to that timelessness where even the notion of birth stays unborn, where time itself is alien.

Braham never was caused—it belongs to the state where causality remains unknown, where causation itself is yet to be caused, where effect is still the unborn orphan. Braham has no origin—it is the realm where even the notion of existence remains nonexistent.

Braham came from nowhere—it is the abiding reality where the ideas of coming and going have no relevance. Braham is the Absolute that always was, always is, will always be.

Braham is the realm called One-Absolute-Consciousness. It has no name but to be able to talk of It we call It Braham. But then again, being of the nature of consciousness, we also call It Him as well.

In the beginning Braham existed within Himself, and within Him was unending bliss. He dwelt within bliss, He emanated bliss, He was bliss itself. Braham ever disports in the mirth that persists e'er ebullient in Him.

Then in the beginning, that Supreme-Being remained motionless and notionless—but even then He was verily the embodiment of Existence, Bliss, Consciousness.

Within Braham was the germ of all knowledge and existences yet to come, but for now Braham remained solitary—His consciousness rife with the knowledge of a billion worlds, but His mind a blank slate in which you and I hitherto remained unwritten.

Aye this was Braham before He became visible in every pore of His creation; and this was the timelessness before the beginning of measurable-space-time.

ॐ

अतः पृथङ्नास्ति जगत्परात्मनः पृथक्प्रतीतिस्तु मृषा गुणादिवत् ।
ataḥ pṛthaṅnāsti jagatparātmanaḥ pṛthakpratītistu mṛṣā guṇādivat ,
आरोपितस्यास्ति किमर्थवत्ताऽधिष्ठानमाभाति तथा भ्रमेण ॥२३५॥
āropitasyāsti kimarthavattā'dhiṣṭhānamābhāti tathā bhrameṇa (VCM-235)

The manifold appearing universe has no existence aside from the singularity of the Absolute: Braham; and the perception of distinctness, separateness, variousness which appears visible within it is illusory—like the appearance of snake in a rope. Does a superimposed attribute have any reality separate from its substratum? It is the substrate which appears to be like the superimposed attribute due to delusion (—like 'blue' is superimposed upon the pristine Space during the day and the 'black' during the night).

Can we envision a consciousness bereft of a body, and of a Beingness, before the beginning of existence itself? Can we conceive of a realm that has no left-right-up-down? Or of existence that has no content? Or of bliss that is not seated in a mind? Or of intelligence that is devoid of thought? Or of a consciousness that has no mind?

That appears well-nigh impossible—for our awareness is much too tainted with the notions of space, time, matter, mind, causation etc. We can not purge our understanding of these very fundamental concepts which permeate every fragment of our awareness. The first question, we are bound to ask is, "Where did this Braham come from?" This question will not arise if we can somehow purge our awareness of all notions—posteriori and a priori.

Such questions arise, because we fail to conceptualize a realm where space, time, and causation do not yet exist. In the visible manifest universe that we see now, we have the laws and standards to compare and judge. Here, causation rules—every thing must have a cause; something must come out of something. Having seen nothing but causation our awareness is so completely tainted with that notion that despite our best mental acrobatics we can not conceive of the Great-Causeless. We can not conceptualize an Absolute Being-ness where none of our laws exist, and where the coming of one out of another simply does not apply. Space, time, causation etc., are all a priori—but which fundamental notions cannot be applied to the Absolute.

The Absolute precedes all law of causation. The Absolute Intelligence just is. He exists. Period. Within the realm of the Absolute, no laws are applicable; therefore, no questions can be raised. How can we apply notions of our universe to a realm that existed before the universe did? How can we raise questions, when we do not know what standards to apply?

And, in this case, none do. Our questions emanate from a frame of reference that is bound under laws of the universe, but we want to apply it to the realm of the Absolute—which is outside all laws. No arguments from within our world can justify the existence of the Absolute. The Absolute exists simply because we know it does. The existence of this universe—which philosophically just boils down to the existence of our own consciousness—and which incidentally is provenly undeniable—attests to the existence of that Absolute.

Unfortunately, when it comes to Braham the Absolute, our minds desert us; they fail to transport us into that realm of pristineness. Our imagination is not fanciful enough, and rightly so—for in this case we have to imagine ourselves purged of all knowledge and notions that taint our awareness. It is convoluted—having to imagine having no mind. At best, we can only surmise.

ॐ

भ्रान्तस्य यद्यद्भ्रमतः प्रतीतं ब्रह्मैव तत्तद्रजतं हि शुक्तिः ।
bhrāntasya yadyadbhramataḥ pratītaṁ brahmaiva tattadrajataṁ hi śuktiḥ ,
इदन्तया ब्रह्म सदैव रूप्यते त्वारोपितं ब्रह्मणि नाममात्रम् ॥ २३६ ॥
idantayā brahma sadaiva rūpyate tvāropitaṁ brahmaṇi nāmamātram (VCM-236)

Through errors and delusions of Nescience, whatever the deluded beings perceive to be a distinct something in the universe—all that is just Braham and Braham alone; all that silvery sheen is indeed only the mother-of-pearl. Braham is ever present as it is, and that which has been superimposed on Braham—the 'Universe'—is merely the diversity of names and forms.

Braham—who is consciousness—is also called *Akshar*, meaning word, also meaning indestructible. The opposite of *Akshar* is *Kshar*, the destructible—the visible form which is seen getting destroyed sooner or later.

Name and form are found connected—a visible form will conjure up its image or name, and a name will conjure up its image. But a form is destructible whereas its name—the idea behind the form—remains indestructible, since it resides within consciousness which abides enduring.

This universe is a form and can be destroyed whereas the idea of that form comes from Braham which is That pure consciousness that can never be destroyed.

As per Ekam-Sanātana-Dharma, Braham and the Universe are intimately connected—they are in fact one and the same; merely two aspects of the same thing. It is the un-manifest Braham who has become manifest into the form of the Cosmos.

Universe is Braham become evolved—and when the universe devolves, it will dissolve back into Braham.

Braham—the un-manifest consciousness; and the Universe—that same consciousness become manifest—are simply two aspects of the same Reality.

All this visible that you see before your eyes—it is all Braham, or God, if you so choose to call Him so—but it is not the notion of god to whose left or right sits a favored son, messenger, prophet through whom he is seen dispensing instructions to humanity. Only Ekam-Sanātana-Dharma has the right definition of God—He is Braham.

Braham is made of two Sanskrit roots: 'Br', meaning bigger or supreme and 'aham' meaning Self. So Braham is the Supreme-Self, i.e. That Supreme-Being within whom this little Self—the being which abides in me as an awareness—is found shining as a little reflection. Ekam-Sanātana-Dharma is the only religion which accurately defines God, by resorting to just one term—the Self, one's consciousness—and which is the only reality that can be attested to and verified. And so the God of Sanātana-Dharma is not only verifiable—because He is fully connected to your Self—but unless you have assayed to so verify that God for yourself directly, then you cannot really be considered religious. Ye, mullaz, priestz, pontiffz, fake-guruz, what right have you to preach of God unless you have directly verified that God for yourself?—so do not simply by yakking inanely of some prophet and book to fool the masses, who abide far higher than ye since atleast they are honest.

Put another way, the Self is a drop of awareness—a consciousness confined; whereas the Supreme-Self is the infinite ocean of consciousness itself—within which abide countless such Selfs.

When, through act of Samādhi, we are able to remove the confinements upon our Self, then we become the Supreme-Self himself, verily a God—and that is what Sanātana-Dharma teaches, and what Ekam-Sanātana-Dharma is all about.

ॐ

आरूढशक्तेरहमो विनाशः कर्तुन्न शक्य सहसापि पण्डितैः ।
ārūḍhaśakterahamo vināśaḥ kartunna śakya sahasāpi paṇḍitaiḥ ,
ये निर्विकल्पाख्यसमाधिनिश्चलाः तानन्तराऽनन्तभवा हि वासनाः ॥ ३४२ ॥
ye nirvikalpākhyasamādhiniścalāḥ tānantarā'nantabhavā hi vāsanāḥ (VCM-342)

Even the learned cannot destroy the egoity of the little 'I' (the confined Self), because it has become strengthened over a lifetime—indeed the ego has become strengthened over myriads of lifetimes by dint of Vāsanās or desires that kept him bound to the world. Verily the dissolution of the 'I', the confined Self, will happen only through the experiencing the Nirvikalpa Samādhi—merging back into Braham, the tranquil ocean from where we once emerged.

Braham—who is absolute-existence, absolute-intelligence, absolute-bliss—describes the Godhead of the Absolute before the beginning of creation.

What was in the beginning? Braham, the pristine infinite Intelligence bereft of thought. What exists now? That same Intelligence—but no longer pristine and which has become evolved into an astronomic thought called the Cosmos.

At the beginning Braham had no thought—and so nothing was visible then. But currently Braham is within an ongoing gargantuan thought—and the visible universe is the concrete shape of that highly complex thought visible before our eyes.

When the seed of knowledge congeals within the Absolute-Intelligence Braham—then it takes the shape of a visible. And it becomes visible to you and me and throughout the universe. How so? Because the projector of the universe as well as the perceiver of the universe, are both He: Braham. At one end He projects; at the other end He perceives.

Braham is the Absolute, which projected this universe by his mere will, and it exists—as, and within everything—as the only abiding reality within all. It abides transcending all the limitations of manifested forms. Undecaying and immutable, Braham is the Absolute realm—of the nature of Infinite Intelligence, Boundless Existence, and Unalloyed Bliss.

Braham is the realm beyond description, without any exemplars. Conceive of Braham as space—indivisible, seamless, and devoid of the notions of cause and effect. Although appearing to be a seeming non-existent void, Braham is the only reality behind all existences. Braham is the one cause behind the cause of all, the only reality behind all activity. It is all pervading and permeates everything; sustaining all, but itself requiring no support.

How to speak of Braham! Truly, Braham has no parallels. It is beyond the bounds of objectification. It is the eternal subject through which all else is known, but which itself stays unknown. The reality of Braham is incomprehensible and unknowable—completely outside the range of sight, speech, mind.

Ever free and a law unto itself, Braham is beyond the jurisdiction of any laws of the world—for all laws emanate from it. It is bound under none, but everything exists fettered to it in bondage. It is the unbounded realm, without a beginning or end, the elixir of Existence, Knowledge and Bliss.

In this universe, there exists just only Braham, the One without a second, the homogeneous realm, devoid of differentiations, with no duality whatsoever. It exists as the only reality within all existences—yet, it is never perceived.

31 The One Consciousness: Braham

Braham is the infinite, eternal, incessant realm within which this universe exists as a dreamlike haze. Howsoever far you may see or imagine, there is only Braham, the One without a second, the unending existence, the abiding sovereignty, which can neither be rejected, nor accepted—for there exists nothing at all that is bereft of Braham.

ॐ

अतः परं ब्रह्म सदद्वितीयं विशुद्धविज्ञानघनं निरञ्जनम् ।
ataḥ paraṁ brahma sadadvitīyaṁ viśuddhavijñānaghanaṁ nirañjanam ,
प्रशान्तमाद्यन्तविहीनमक्रियं निरन्तरानन्दरसस्वरूपम् ॥२३७॥
praśāntamādyantavihīnamakriyaṁ nirantarānandarasasvarūpam (VCM-237)

Whatever appears to be manifested is nothing but the Supreme Braham Itself—the Real, non-dual, arrantly pure, taintless, supremely serene, without a beginning, without an end, beyond activity, and ever of the essence of absolute Knowledge and Bliss.

And, what is your relationship to Braham? You yourself are that Braham. That whom you worship as God, is the real you—and of which this body and mind are but mere distorted reflections.

You are the Supreme Braham, the One without a second, who is of the nature of Eternal Existence, Infinite Intelligence, and Boundless Bliss. You are Braham, and nothing else besides.

ॐ

ज्ञातृज्ञेयज्ञानशून्यमनन्तं निर्विकल्पकम् ।
jñātṛjñeyajñānaśūnyamanantaṁ nirvikalpakam ,
केवलाखण्डचिन्मात्रं परं तत्त्वं विदुर्बुधाः ॥२३९॥
kevalākhaṇḍacinmātraṁ paraṁ tattvaṁ vidurbudhāḥ (VCM-239)

That supreme Being Braham—in whom there are no differentiations such as knower, knowledge and known; who is infinite, transcendent, and the essence of Knowledge Absolute—is directly realized within as one's very own Self by the Yogi.

That, which is the substratum of the universe, which supports all, which is the cause of the projection, maintenance, and dissolution of the worlds, which is devoid of all duality, and is infinite and indestructible—verily you are That Braham.

That, which is free from birth and death, increase and decrease, waste and disease; which is imperishable; which even Time, the all destroyer, can not annihilate—that Deathless Reality is you.

That, beyond which there is nothing, which exists in all, which shines in every direction and permeates all things, which reverberates through every fragment of creation; whose essence is Existence-Intelligence-Bliss Absolute, eternal and immutable—that Supreme Braham you are.

That, which is beyond religion and creed, family and lineage; which is devoid of names and forms, merits and demerits; which is free from all differentiations; which transcends space, time, matter and causation—that Timeless Existence is the very essence of your being.

Aye, you are none other than Braham, the only abiding reality, constant and immutable. You are that indestructible reality which can never die, which can not be burnt, which can not be slain, which can not be drowned. This is the absolute truth about your nature—you are verily God, the Supreme Being, the Creator of this Universe—if you dare to accept this bold truth of Ekam-Sanātana-Dharma.

ॐ

मृत्कार्यं सकलं घटादि सततं मृन्मात्रमेवाहितं
mṛtkāryaṁ sakalaṁ ghaṭādi satataṁ mṛnmātramevāhitaṁ
तद्वत्सज्जनितं सदात्मकमिदं सन्मात्रमेवाखिलम् ।
tadvatsajjanitaṁ sadātmakamidaṁ sanmātramevākhilam ,
यस्मान्नास्ति सतः परं किमपि तत्सत्यं स आत्मा स्वयं
yasmānnāsti sataḥ paraṁ kimapi tatsatyaṁ sa ātmā svayaṁ
तस्मात्तत्त्वमसि प्रशान्तममलं ब्रह्माद्वयं यत्परम् ॥ २५१ ॥
tasmāttattvamasi praśāntamamalaṁ brahmādvayaṁ yatparam (VCM-251)

All modifications of the clay—such as pots etc., which are always accepted by the mind to be real—are in fact nothing but clay; similarly this here entire Cosmos, which is produced from Braham, is Braham Itself and nothing but Braham. Being that there exists nothing else whatsoever besides Braham, the only self-existent Reality, which is our very own Self. So then verily thou too art That—the serene, the pure, the supreme Braham, the One without a second.

EKAM-SANĀTANA-DHARMA

Vidyā-putra Veni-prasād, a wandering sadhu from a kali-yuga of two billion years ago, is on a pilgrimage and has stopped at a village to rest. Here he is talking to people sitting under a banyan tree. Vidyā-putra said: "

What is Ekam-Sanātana-Dharma?

Ekam Sanātana-Dharma is an edifice—a compendium of principles, rules, disciplines—which has as its foundation one supreme Truth: that there abides just One-Being in existence, Braham. And living under the aegis of Sanātana-Dharma, humans—as individuals and collectively as humanity—can coexist, together and with the world, in harmony and happiness. Most importantly, following its Yogic disciplines, an individual gains the ability to attain the seat of supreme bliss whenever he is ready and chooses to make a go for it.

Being that it has as its foundation the Truth of Braham—which is the only eternal Reality—Ekam-Sanātana-Dharma too is eternal: not confined to place, time, people, language. Even billion of years hereafter or before, even on planets billions of light-years away, even amongst civilizations anywhere in the cosmos which are completely different from us humans, this exact Ekam-Sanātana-Dharma will prevail. Why you ask? Because it is woven around the truth of One Reality Braham—He who pervades the entirety of the universe—and that can never change, and so therefore Sanātana-Dharma abides eternal; it is as inviolate as the laws of the universe.

Ekam-Sanātana-Dharma is the haven of humans and humanity—should we choose to embrace it—and following on its footsteps we get not only worldly happiness but also spiritual felicity in the form of supernal bliss—the highest treasure compared to which rest everything of the world is heaps of bones, skins, dust, ashes.

Importantly whichever race or society manages to ingrain and bind Ekam-Sanātana-Dharma in their framework, their perpetual existence is ensured—so long as they are sincere in their effort to preserve and uphold it with bravery and without shying—unlike the derisory Zindoos of today.

That the oldest civilization of the world—of Āryāvarta, or Bhārat (Zindia now)—still remains extant to some extent, when all other ancient world civilizations are dead and gone, is by purely by dint of Ekam-Sanātana-Dharma, which divine endowment was bestowed unto them by Braham Rāma, and which became woven into their fabric many millenniums ago, and it has nothing at all to do with that race itself—which unfortunately underwent a transformation for the worse these past two-three millenniums and thereby became utterly lazy, easygoing, stupid, cowering—whose leadership couldn't manage to fight for their life, honor, women, symbols, temples; whose people became so bedazed that they just remained cringing in a huddle and were slaughtered by the hundreds of millions or converted by Zizlamists, rather than stand firm and fight those barbarians; which people, though invariably in majority, always persisted remaining ruled by a handful of aggressive barbaric encroachers and invaders with missionary zeal—even down to the present times, still sucking up to Zizlamists minority to stay alive at their mercy, still being ruled under the Zenglishman's derived ideals, ideas, constitution, education, laws, codes, standards, dress, mannerism, ways, everything – even when they are ostensibly independent – not embracing or introducing into their constitution and laws even one of the Sanātana principles which in fact remain as the very foundation of world civilization—shows the power innate in Ekam-Sanātana-Dharma, which alone has saved this race from complete annihilation thus far; because you see Ekam-Sanātana-Dharma carries with it Sītā-Rāma's very own blessings, and these people's ancestors did serve Sanātana-Dharma so well for initial many millenniums—with the rot beginning in just the past two-three millenniums and now ripened to full maturity these past eighty-three years since Zindia's so-called Independence.

Sanātana-Dharma is rapidly dying within Zindia and it appears that this great religion can no longer be entrusted to survive on the incapable shoulders of these debile people—most of whom are the Macullūs, the mental progeny of Lord Macaulay—and perhaps Rāma will likely shift that responsibility somewhere else—to a people or nation more capable.

Going forward, whichever nation, race, or people will manage to inculcate Ekam-Sanātana-Dharma within their midst and practice it sincerely, then do know that Sītā-Rāma's own benedictions comes along with that, and they will be saved despite their many modest faults, and they will be protected even through a BROB event—the Big-Reset-Of-Braham, which incidentally will be arriving at the world's doorsteps quite soon.

Oh I am so caught in this world of Māyā;
O elysian-one, I so much miss the bliss of thine.
Far yon in those azure deeps
thou linger,
hid within thy golden lights;
but I, alas, just sleep sleep sleep.

And in my slumber I hear an eager voice calling out;
it's a Rishi of yore trying to say something to me,
his eyes agleam bright and warm,
but his brows are so sad—with a single tear standing in the corner of his eye;
and in the accent of an ancient unknown tongue,
his voice intones like a silver clarion being rung,
and having said what he had to say to me,
in the end he sends a warning in urgent words:
O human,
the ravine where thou sleep is steep and deep,
the darkness is lowering and a tempest right overhead;

O dreamer of the summer nights, great danger awaits thee;
O thou dreaming in these slumbering lights, just arise,
O wake up friend, I do plead.

But I, alas; I just sleep; I just sleep.
The foolish human just sleeps, sleeps, sleeps
—asleep to the BROB event waiting on the horizon.

In future another nation, people, race could wake up to the enormity of Sanātana-Dharma—of her majestic resplendency, of not just her science and practicality but her profound sublime beauty—and adopt Ekam-Sanātana-Dharma passionately. When that happens the burden will have shifted, and Zindia's doom will become firmly sealed with that event—reduced completely to a nation of slavish imitators, which they already are but a thin mantle of Sanātana-Dharma draped upon them saves them from complete ignominy for now.

Despite their irremissible sins of uncaring indolent craven slovenly existence, the fact that the Zindoos survived so far was all thanks to the blessing of Sanātana-Dharma which still lightly rests upon their heads. How long their future survival will continue is a big question because these past eighty-three years since they supposedly became independent, these people—now rendered conditioned into Macullūs, Lord Macaulay's children—have abandoned Sanātana-Dharma en-masse, leaving her by the droves to become wannabe Zenglishmen and Zenglishwomen.

Unless of course He chooses to bring on HROB, the Huge-Reset—Braham will likely wish to keep Sanātana-Dharma still entrenched within human society, to give humanity hope and a chance; and millenniums ago Braham had chosen the people of Zindia for that very express task: that of preserving and disseminating Sanātana-Dharma but to which onerous responsibility they have failed miserably, especially these past few milleniums; and now the writing is on the wall and another more deserving people could be chosen by Rāma to carry out that divine task.

The Sanskrit word Sanātana means eternal—that which is ever there, requiring no props—which is self-existent and undying. The word Dharma is derived from the root Dhāran—that which holds like a foundation, the fundament which bears and supports all that which will exist on its top. Dharma is that inner core upon which can exist the outer—and which inner when deformed or weakened, deforms and weakens the outer structure as well.

It is only Braham who is the ultimate understructure, the fundament upon which the entire universe stands supported; and since Braham does the Dhāran of the whole universe—so it is Braham only which is one's supreme Dharma. And that is the reason why, according to Sanātana-Dharma, our ultimate Dharma is all about finding our oneness in Braham upon whom we abide held extant.

Sanātana-Dharma is eternal—it was, and will always remain abiding—even if the bearers and carriers of Sanātana-Dharma and the language on which it is borne, were to vanish away. Humans can disappear tomorrow but Sanātana-Dharma will still persist eternal—because it embodies the Great-Truth: the Truth about the this universe and the supreme Being who stands behind it—which truth can never change. Period.

If humans and all their knowledge were to disappear, a new dance of creation will play out on earth—and with it, new life and new species; and then—even a billion years from now—those novel creatures are bound to stumble upon the Truth of the exact same Sanātana-Dharma of which you read here—albeit proclaimed in a different tongue then, and by a different bearer of the Sanātana-Dharma at that time. That is why the great Rishis of Bharat have declared that Sanātana-Dharma is eternal—just as Braham, the supreme consciousness, abides eternal.

Just like gravity is an eternal truth—whether discovered or not, whether embodied in languages and laws and equations, or not—Sanātana-Dharma is the eternal Truth which proclaims that there is just this One-Ocean-of-Consciousness, and this Cosmos—all these multitudes of names and forms—are merely the various manifestations of That-One-Consciousness. And although we may right now think that we are a body and a mind, but when we subject our consciousness to intense scrutiny and discipline, then we shall discover that we are really the Lord-God Himself—we are That-Being who created this universe, who stands pervading it, who is behind each and everything that exists.

Ekam-Sanātana-Dharma is not a "religion" in the sense of how the word religion is used in prevalent times, but since no alternate word exists, you can choose to call Sanātana-Dharma a religion—if you insist on naming names. Be cognizant though at all times that Sanātana-Dharma is a "religion" that exists self-existent—on its own, standing on its own merits, bereft of bolsters and props, requiring no shoring up, without any special prophet, god, men, women—without even any human to remain pertinent—because it embodies the eternal truth which will always found to be true—even a billion years from now: that you and I and this universe—all this existence—is just One-Consciousness become manifest.

And all these various rules and rituals—the Do's and Don'ts of Sanātana-Dharma—are merely for us to decimate our delusions and attain to our true state—that of attaining our Oneness in Braham, becoming the embodiment of Bliss—should we so choose. And we humans do not necessarily have to follow the path of Sanātana-Dharma—it is perfectly okay from Braham's perspective.

There are absolutely no compulsions in Sanātana-Dharma. Unlike other religions, there is no God here playing carrots and sticks—and blaming it all on devil and satan or on the man himself for "straying" away every time those religion zealots fail to come up with an answer and have to resort to hand waving—which is mostly most of the time.

The religion of Sanātana-Dharma is not few crafty priestz, pontiffz, mullaz preying upon the weak and gullible. There is no god here doling out dictates that come to humanity only via his favored son, messenger, prophet; no little book dispensing instructions how best to slaughter animals to eat; no having to cower before a man blindly so he can put in a good word for us on the day of judgment; no going up and down on the ground and rotating the neck facing a certain direction with loudspeaker blaring full blast several times a day; no having to accept a man as my savior or else be damned—no it is none of that. The religion of Sanātana-Dharma is all about getting out of this terrible suffering of life and death, and attaining the totality of bliss in this very life while we live.

If religion doesn't bring us felicity while we live and makes golden promises of paradise only if we remain controlled by their little book and stay as good boys, of what avail is it other than helping the priestz and mullaz perpetrating a sham for their own benefits?

In Sanātana-Dharma, we are free to completely reject Dharma and live life as it comes—and suffer the joys and pains which the world throws at us. Braham, the God of Sanātana-Dharma, is perfectly content to whichsoever path humans and humanity choose to follow—because unto Braham this is all a sport, a play, and we are all actors on His stage, and moreover we all are He Himself.

If as individual humans we choose to spurn Ekam-Sanātana-Dharma with disdain, then we will continue to revolve in this world of joys and sorrows in an endless cycle—it is as inevitable as any Law-of-Nature. Further if the collective humanity chooses to reject Sanātana-Dharma, then human society will stand destroyed, human species will disappear from earth—and then Jivas will only have the lower life forms available to be reborn on earth for Braham's ongoing sport—as was happening for millions of years before human forms came into existence.

We are just another of earth's creature—except that we are far ahead on the evolution scale, and given time, other creatures too will get there—after we are gone. So in our arrogance of materialism, let's not get too haughty, for we can easily be destroyed tomorrow if we do not respect life, soul, consciousness that is rife throughout the universe everywhere.

Enjoying luxuries untold, and upbeat eudemonia,
proliferating on earth like uncontained bacteria,
fat, breathless, with too much to eat,
puffed breathless in our pride and hauteur,
this dominion of earth is entirely ours to take, rape,
and it is our prerogative to decide—
whether to let things live, or bring them death,
just stretch out our hands and pluck out anyone and anything,
aye, Arrogant Humans is our first and last name.

But alas, this is so long as we do not meet,
our greater contender face to face:
King-Annihilation—
who will be discovered to be our very own offspring.

Follow Sanātana-Dharma, or your own merry ways, Braham—the God of Sanātana-Dharma—does not really care either way. And if in their folly humans were to destroy themselves, Braham has infinite time and infinite creativity and He will be perfectly content in innovating brand new creatures—even far more fantastic than these ones here.

Aye, the God of Ekam-Sanātana-Dharma enforces no compulsions on anyone. Yes, he did bestow on humanity the great endowment of Sanātana-Dharma, and He would be happy if we live by our Dharma, but that God is perfectly content if humans follow Adharma and its ensuing pains—His Creation would go on just fine.

However some hope is held out to humans through this verse which Lord-God Krishna says in the Bhagavad-Gītā:

— ॐ —

परित्राणाय साधूनां विनाशाय च दुष्कृताम् ।
paritrāṇāya sādhūnāṁ vināśāya ca duṣkṛtām
धर्मसंस्थापनार्थाय सम्भवामि युगे युगे ॥४-८॥
dharmasaṁsthāpanārthāya sambhavāmi yuge yuge (BG-4-8)

For the protection of the righteous, and for the destruction of the evil, and for the establishment of Dharma upon earth, I take advent from Age to Age.

But 'Age' is a very long time—it could be many millenniums, even hundreds of, before the Avatar of Vishnu takes advent on earth again, so do not hold your breath; it is better if we ourselves learn our lessons and mend our ways well in time.

In-fact if we humans end up destroying ourselves and all the earth creatures—aye, a Huge-Reset appears more probable than a BROB, considering the insanity of Adharma plaguing the world today—then our Creator would be perfectly happy to spin afresh a newly dance of creation—at the end of which would exist other species, perhaps more intelligent and better behaved than we monkey-offsprings, through which He will continue with His sport.

So the burden is upon us; it behooves us humans—both as individuals and as collective—to pursue a life aligned with the principles of Sanātana-Dharma; it is in our own selfish interest that we follow the path of Sanātana-Dharma to avoid collective and individual pain. In Braham's scheme of things, Ekam-Sanātana-Dharma is delineated simply as the preferred way to avoid present and future anguishes, and is by no means a compulsion.

With the purpose of attaining our innate state—that of eternal bliss—to become one with our origin, our essence—broadly two paths have been delineated in

Sanātana-Dharma: Pravritti-Mārg and the Nivritti-Mārg. And following these paths, the soot which is covering our Ātmā washes away and then we come by eternal bliss—our true essence.

Karma-Yoga, Bhakti-Yoga, Jnāna-Yoga, Rāja-Yoga are the different disciplines of these paths. We can realize our true nature following any of the Yogas of Sanātana-Dharma—Yoga means to become yoked back to the Supreme, in whom we have our origin but which roots now stand forgotten.

We shall talk some more on this topic in future books, but for now know that Pravritti-Mārg is for those who live in lockstep with the world—notably these are the householders, of the Grahastha Āshram. The Pravritti way focuses more on Karma-Yoga and Bhakti-Yoga and less on Jnāna-Yoga and Rāja-Yoga. By contrast Nivritti-Mārg is for those who have completely renounced the world—those in the Sanyāsa Āshram; the main emphasis there being on Jnāna-Yoga and Rāja-Yoga.

Scriptures like the Bhagavad-Gītā and the Rāmāyana cover the entirety of Sanātana-Dharma and they cover both the Māargas but are particularly well suited for those in the Pravritti-Mārg.

Pravritti-Mārg means the path oriented towards the world, and Nivritti-Mārg is the path oriented away from the world. These are also sometimes called the path of Karma-Bhakti-Yoga and the path of Sānkhya-Yoga respectively. Though appearing very divergent, but they lead to the same outcome—with the aspirant on either path eventually attaining to Braham.

A householder, who follows the Pravritti-Mārg of Karma-Bhakti Yogas, reaches the exact same beatitude as reached by the all- renouncing Sanyāsi, who follows the Nivritti-Mārg of Jnāna-Rāja Yogas. The former way—that of the householders—being much easier in its practices, is often the preferred choice of most people. Those who renounce the world in pursuit of Braham are quite rare. But both paths lead to the same destination, and in Sanātana-Dharma—the beautiful religion without compulsions—people are encouraged to follow the path that is in line with their inner nature and their situation in life.

— ॐ —

संन्यासः कर्मयोगश्च निःश्रेयसकरावुभौ ।
saṁnyāsaḥ karmayogaśca niḥśreyasakarāvubhau
तयोस्तु कर्मसंन्यासात्कर्मयोगो विशिष्यते ॥५-२॥
tayostu karmasaṁnyāsātkarmayogo viśiṣyate (BG-5-2)

Sanyāsa—the complete renunciation of action; and Karma-Yoga—the physical performance of duty but renouncing it mentally: they are both good and lead to emancipation. Of the two however, the path of Karma-Yoga—being easier to practice—is deemed superior.

— ॐ —

साङ्ख्ययोगौ पृथग्बालाः प्रवदन्ति न पण्डिताः ।
sāṅkhyayogau pṛthagbālāḥ pravadanti na paṇḍitāḥ
एकमप्यास्थितः सम्यगुभयोर्विन्दते फलम् ॥५-४॥
ekamapyāsthitaḥ samyagubhayorvindate phalam (BG-5-4)

It is the ignorant who perceives Sānkhya-Yoga and Karma-Yoga as leading to different outcomes—but not so the wise. Firmly established in even one, one obtains the fruit of both.

— ॐ —

यत्साङ्ख्यैः प्राप्यते स्थानं तद्योगैरपि गम्यते ।
yatsāṅkhyaiḥ prāpyate sthānaṁ tadyogairapi gamyate
एकं साङ्ख्यं च योगं च यः पश्यति स पश्यति ॥५-५॥
ekaṁ sāṅkhyaṁ ca yogaṁ ca yaḥ paśyati sa paśyati (BG-5-5)

That sovereign state which is reached by the Sānkhya-Yogī, is attained by the Karma-Yogī as well. He who sees the Path of Jnāna and the Path of Karma-Yoga (duty-driven work) to be one and the same, he truly sees.

Jiva in Birth-Death Cycle

Vidyā-putra Veni-prasād, a wandering sadhu from a kali-yuga of two billion years ago, is on a pilgrimage and has stopped at a village to rest. Here he is talking to people sitting under a banyan tree. Vidyā-putra said: "

— ॐ —

बहूनि मे व्यतीतानि जन्मानि तव चार्जुन ।
bahūni me vyatītāni janmāni tava cārjuna
तान्यहं वेद सर्वाणि न त्वं वेत्थ परन्तप ॥४-५॥
tānyahaṁ veda sarvāṇi na tvaṁ vettha parantapa (BG-4-5)

[Lord-God Krishna says:] "Many a lives have I lived, O Arjuna—you too as well; I know them all but you remember them not, O chastiser of foes.

— ॐ —

As the Jivas of the world, we have been revolving in the birth-death cycle for eons, and this birth we have is the latest episode in a long, long drama full of pleasures, love, spouses, children, revelry, melodrama, mundane, tragedy, troubles, battles, comedy, pains, sorrows, delights, desire, lust, hurts, inflictions, lechery, euphoria, disease, and reigning or slaving variously, playing different roles in our countless human lives; or just undergoing the intense fight for survival, living as the unnumbered fishes, birds, beasts of the world.

A panoptic view of our entire journey from endless ages will turn up to be one burdensome, cumbersome, wretched existence with more dreary and dismal than bright and colorful; more dark and sinister than cheering and inspiring; with much more pains than joys—and the wise person very early on decides that he has had enough of this and that and that he needs to get out of this terrible transmigratory cycle right away.

O I still can remember,
how the seas were so severe, stormy, rough,
how Māyā's winds kept sweeping at me,
kept dredging me down,
me held weighed under Time's crushing rolls.
I still can see my countless different bodies,

tossing, threshing, turning,
upon roaring tempest-waves,
heaped upon the worldly ocean like so many carcasses,
with the crushing weight of all those bodies,
still weighing so deeply upon my soul.

And how many, many were the terrible tempests
bursting, sweltering, leaping, raging
in those countless different lives;
how mighty and cruel were Karma's arms
repeatedly throwing at me destiny's hard knocks—
sharp and severe like so many rocks.

Millenniums come and they go
—and centuries roll by as like minutes—
and my soul has turned so dark and so cold;
and my limbs are now so weary and so sore—
and even having to have these fresh garbs of new bodies,
has become now so jaded and so old!
O, I must get out of this birth-death cycle this time around—
I have to, have to, have to!
So help me Lord God Sītā-Rāma,
just get me the hell out of this worldly hell,
when the body falls off this time.

ॐ

ताभ्यां प्रवर्धमाना सा सूते संसृतिमात्मनः ।
tābhyāṁ pravardhamānā sā sūte saṁsṛtimātmanaḥ ,
त्रयाणां च क्षयोपायः सर्वावस्थासु सर्वदा ॥३१५॥
trayāṇāṁ ca kṣayopāyaḥ sarvāvasthāsu sarvadā (VCM-315)
सर्वत्र सर्वतः सर्वब्रह्ममात्रावलोकनैः ।
sarvatra sarvataḥ sarvabrahmamātrāvalokanaiḥ ,
सद्भाववासनादार्ढ्यात्तत्त्रयं लयमश्नुते ॥३१६॥
sadbhāvavāsanādārḍhyāttattrayaṁ layamaśnute (VCM-316)

Pulled in the vicious circle of Activity and Desire, the soul revolves in unending Transmigration—a perpetual cycle of births, deaths, sorrows. The way to destroy this tricycle lies in looking upon everything as Braham and Braham alone—throughout, under all circumstance, ever and in every respect. With the strengthening of the longing to become One in Braham, these three are thereby destroyed.

ॐ

बुद्धौ गुहायां सदसद्विलक्षणं ब्रह्मास्ति सत्यं परमद्वितीयम् ।
buddhau guhāyāṁ sadasadvilakṣaṇaṁ brahmāsti satyaṁ paramadvitīyam ,
तदात्मना योऽत्र वसेद्गुहायां पुनर्न तस्याङ्गगुहाप्रवेशः ॥२६६॥
tadātmanā yo'tra vasedguhāyāṁ punarna tasyāṅgaguhāpraveśaḥ (VCM-266)

⌘

In the cave of the *Buddhi* abides Braham—the Supreme non-dual Reality, the One without a second, distinct from the gross and subtle. For one who dwells in this cave in complete identity with Braham, there is no more the pain, horror, sorrow of having to dwell in any mother's womb in future.

We act and the nature reacts upon us; if we do good then it will come back to us, and if we do bad then that too comes back to us—eventually.

We say "eventually" because the fruit of our karma may not fructify in this life but in a future one—at a time when the environment for it to ripen become just right, and then destiny will hand to us those fruits on a platter and force them down our throats whether we like it or not. We will eventually get what we have sown—good or bad—although it might happen in some future life. The inexplicable events of our this life—pleasant or unpleasant—are just fruits of our past karmas bearing fruits.

Throughout our existence over the eons we, the Jivas, have been revolving in the birth-death cycle of the world, doing all sorts of insanely good and crazy bad things, and enjoying and suffering as a consequence of the Law-of-Karma.

Sanātana-Dharma has a number of distinctive features and one of them is the theory of Karma which essentially posits that every action begets a reaction. Just like the laws of physics which govern cause and effect, action and reaction, there is this ineluctable Law-of-Karma applicable to Jiva's existence which states that we all must eventually harvest what we had sown—be it good or bad. Every action of ours will have an effect consequent to it; if we commit sinful acts, then we shall pay the penalties thence; and if we do virtuous acts then we shall reap the rewards thereof.

According to Sanātana-Dharma one of the reasons the Jiva is born again and again is to experience the consequences of deeds done—good and bad; the other reason is seeking to fulfill unfulfilled desires and pursue unrealized dreams of our many past lives—including what we will end up accumulating in this one. With more desires and attachments we forge with people in this life—that is just so many more births and pain-joy experiences that we are burdening ourselves with, and they keep propelling us forward in this seemingly endless journey of ours.

The effect always ensues—if not in this life then in some future life; and so the inexplicable sufferings we undergo in this life must have been fruits of some past Karma of ours—which just happen to have found the right environment to play out now in order to become exhausted.

And yes, happiness too will come of its own, even without striving—if it's the time for those karmas to bear fruits. Consider this: No one wants unhappiness, we keep evading it in a thousand ways, and yet it comes and perforce clings to us—because of some past karma bearing fruit. Similarly joys and delights will come whether we want them or not—they will necessarily come and take us in their embrace, whether or not we try for them—because these are our past karmas bearing fruits and being forced down upon us by Karma's laws.

Recognizing that there is a cause-effect prevalent in whatever we do, Sanātana-Dharma advocates "Do good; do no evil... etc." Such exhortations are dispersed throughout our various texts. However the best thing—as the Bhagavad-Gītā advocates—is to just go beyond both good and bad and perform Karmas in a spirit of detachment, offering them all as an oblation to Braham.

— ॐ —

कर्मजं बुद्धियुक्ता हि फलं त्यक्त्वा मनीषिणः ।
karmajaṁ buddhiyuktā hi phalaṁ tyaktvā manīṣiṇaḥ
जन्मबन्धविनिर्मुक्ताः पदं गच्छन्त्यनामयम् ॥२-५१॥
janmabandhavinirmuktāḥ padaṁ gacchantyanāmayam (BG-2-51)

Endowed with the wisdom of equanimity, and abandoning attachments to the fruits born of action, the Karma-Yogī is thereby freed of the shackles of births and deaths and attains to self-realization—ascending to that supreme Abode which is void of all sorrows.

The Jiva is born time and again in order to exhaust his bag of Karmas. The wise person therefore does nothing—abides in equanimity—accumulating no karmas good or bad—this is the way of Jnāna, which is rather hard. Alternately, in whatever work he performs, he first makes it as an offering to the Lord-God—as enjoined in the Bhagavad-Gītā; and that way nothing good or bad accrues to him ever—this is the easier way of Bhakti and Karma.

— ॐ —

कृतं न कति जन्मानि कायेन मनसा गिरा ।
kṛtaṁ na kati janmāni kāyena manasā girā ,
दुःखमायासदं कर्म तदद्याप्युपरम्यताम् ॥१०-८॥
duḥkhamāyāsadaṁ karma tadadyāpyuparamyatām (AG-10-8)

— ॐ —

In how many unnumbered births
have you not suffered harsh painful labor
of the body, mind, speech?
Desist even now.
In this life at least just let it all cease
—and come by peace!
Just abide poised in equanimousness.

Our emancipation within everlasting bliss is in finding our inmost essence, the Ātmā, using the paths of Ekam-Sanātana-Dharma called Yogas—meaning union, to become yoked to the Supreme, the methods following which we gain Self-realization—and of which paths there are several like: Jnāna-Yoga, Karma-Yoga, Bhaktī-Yoga, Rāja-Yoga etc.

BHAKTI-YOGA

Vidyā-putra Veni-prasād, a wandering sadhu from a kali-yuga of two billion years ago, is on a pilgrimage and has stopped at a village to rest. Here he is talking to people sitting under a banyan tree. Vidyā-putra said: "

In the Rāmacharitmānasa we see how we the Jivas are caught in Māyā's delusion with our minds firmly entrenched in her deluding enchantments, and the way out is not easy to see. One way is the path of Jnāna but that path is quite hard—and so too are some other paths; moreover if destiny too conspires against us and complicates our life then our way out to freedom becomes even far rougher and knottier. So what is the way out?

— ॐ —

ईस्वर अंस जीव अबिनासी । चेतन अमल सहज सुखरासी ॥
īsvara aṁsa jīva abināsī, cetana amala sahaja sukharāsī.
सो मायाबस भयउ गोसाईं । बँध्यो कीर मरकट की नाईं ॥
so māyābasa bhayau gosāīṁ, baṁdhyo kīra marakaṭa kī nāīṁ.
जड़ चेतनहि ग्रंथि परि गई । जदपि मृषा छूटत कठिनई ॥
jaṛa cetanahi graṁthi pari gaī, jadapi mṛṣā chūṭata kaṭhinaī.
तब ते जीव भयउ संसारी । छूट न ग्रंथि न होइ सुखारी ॥
taba te jīva bhayau saṁsārī, chūṭa na graṁthi na hoi sukhārī.
श्रुति पुरान बहु कहेउ उपाई । छूट न अधिक अधिक अरुझाई ॥
śruti purāna bahu kaheu upāī, chūṭa na adhika adhika arujhāī.

The Jiva is a particle of the divinity—immortal, intelligent, pure and innately replete with bliss; but being overcome by Māyā, he is caught in the world—just like parrots and monkeys become ensnared into captivity through their greed. The Jiva—though of the nature of pure consciousness—remains captive, held bound in Māyā's knots difficult to untie although supposedly delusive. Thus the Jiva, who is of the nature of divine, has become earthly bound; there is no loosing of knots and happiness ever eludes him. Although for emancipation, the Vedas and Purānas have declared many remedies, but still there is no getting release—rather for the Jiva these worldly entanglements keep increasing. (RCM-7)

One way out of the pains and travails of the world is the beautiful path of Bhakti that comes to us so naturally. Bhakti-Yoga is quest for Braham-Rāma and, wonders of wonders, in that path those very things—i.e., the body, sense-organs, mind—are utilized to aid us which are normally obstructive to Truth and considered impediments to self-realization in other paths. Instead of curbing the sense-organs and mind—as enjoined in the Rāja-Yoga for instance—the Bhakta employs the strategy of squarely placing his God to wheresoever the sense-organs and mind stray to.

Within the human heart, Love abides as a natural impulsion for union: becoming one, make that my own. And although it often becomes a great cause of our misery when directed towards earthly beings and things—which by nature are are evanescent, changeful, infidel—but when the same love is directed towards its proper mark—which can only be God because in Him alone exists infinite bliss—then it brings us deliverance.

Ah human love!
One should laugh, for it makes one cry.
It begins full of sweets & hearts & loves & passion & pledges,
but there is always something wanting, something amiss;
and soon it starts to crumble, wither, harden—then just dies,
before turning around 180
to become a pledge for sweet revenge.

Aye, human love only brings troubles and pains,
and memories of lost love ever haunt our minds,
and there's ever more suffering and even more despair—
'aye, I am a human but in name—likely I am a worm, but surely
a wretched idiot'—we thus think as we wring our hands;
and we eat many a bitter fruit of regrets,
and with just snares and scoffs as our company,
we seek respite in dark corners to evade life's stress,
but nothing really recompenses us for our sorrows and lost
years.

Treading life's dismal wilderness,
with no smile to cheer, no voices to bless,
just restless sleep of tossing and turning,
and an unending dark night that shows
no hint of approaching morning—
such is the usual culmination of most human unions

that are supposedly made in heaven.

By that one act of human love—nay betrayal,
for that is what human love really has become,
the divinity of my nature, is now rendered forfeited forever;
and my heart has become filled with nameless despair,
and maybe I should just press the Del-key of Self-destruct;
aye, that is what human love has came down to—
although the love of parents is an exception here.

It is only God who alone can reciprocate our love with full fidelity. After all Sītā-Rāma is the Ocean of Bliss and He is all-capable; and so it should be no wonder then that He is the one whom the devotee chooses to offer his highest love—which is Bhakti, or devotion— offered unto our Lord-God, the embodiment of perfect bliss, love, compassion.

To fall in love with the visible and beautiful is a natural propensity of the mind—love in some form or other is the easy-most, pleasant-most, and natural-most human trait—and the Bhakta puts that trait to full use by taking a beautiful form he has become attracted to and considers that to be the Lord-God Himself; and he begins to love and venerate Braham in that very form. Gradually he works his way to complete oneness with the Supreme through that love and devotion. When a devotee offers worship to Rāma, he sees pristineness, bliss, almightiness of Braham that has become embodied in Sītā-Rāma. Unlike the other paths, the path of Bhakti is most natural, beautiful, easy, pleasant.

— ॐ —

ग्यान पंथ कृपान कै धारा । परत खगेस होइ नहिं बारा ॥
gyāna paṁtha kṛpāna kai dhārā, parata khagesa hoi nahiṁ bārā.
जो निर्बिघ्न पंथ निर्बहई । सो कैवल्य परम पद लहई ॥
jo nirbighna paṁtha nirbahaī, so kaivalya parama pada lahaī.
अति दुर्लभ कैवल्य परम पद । संत पुरान निगम आगम बद ॥
ati durlabha kaivalya parama pada, saṁta purāna nigama āgama bada.
राम भजत सोइ मुकुति गोसाईं । अनइच्छित आवइ बरिआईं ॥
rāma bhajata soi mukuti gosāīṁ, anaicchita āvai bariāīṁ.
जिमि थल बिनु जल रहि न सकाई । कोटि भाँति कोउ करै उपाई ॥

jimi thala binu jala rahi na sakāī, koṭi bhāṁti kou karai upāī.

तथा मोच्छ सुख सुनु खगराई । रहि न सकइ हरि भगति बिहाई ॥

tathā moccha sukha sunu khagarāī, rahi na sakai hari bhagati bihāī.

अस बिचारि हरि भगत सयाने । मुक्ति निरादर भगति लुभाने ॥

asa bicāri hari bhagata sayāne, mukti nirādara bhagati lubhāne.

भगति करत बिनु जतन प्रयासा । संसृति मूल अबिद्या नासा ॥

bhagati karata binu jatana prayāsā, saṁsṛti mūla abidyā nāsā.

भोजन करिअ तृपिति हित लागी । जिमि सो असन पचवै जठरागी॥

bhojana karia tṛpiti hita lāgī, jimi so asana pacavai jaṭharāgī.

असि हरि भगति सुगम सुखदाई । को अस मूढ़ न जाहि सोहाई ॥

asi hari bhagati sugama sukhadāī, ko asa mūṛha na jāhi sohāī.

The path of Wisdom is like the edge of a scimitar; for those who step on it, O Garud, there is little escape. If any traverse the path in spite of its difficulty, they attain to the supreme sphere of beatitude, no doubt. But this exalted felicity is immensely hard of attainment—as declared by saints, Purānas, Vedas and other scriptures. Now contrast this with Devotion: By the worship of Rāma, O sir, that same beatitude comes freely of its own accord. As water cannot stay secured without some container, however much you may try to make it, in like manner, O Garud, the joy of final salvation cannot be secured without the worship of Harī. The wisest of Harī's worshippers know this; and rebuffing emancipation they much rather crave for Bhakti. By Devotion, without any trouble or difficulty, the ignorance that arises from mundane existence is utterly destroyed with no effort on our part—just like we eat for our gratification and make only that effort, but the digestion happens automatically, on its own without a conscious exertion. What fool is there who does not welcome such an easy path of Devotion to Rāma—which path is simultaneously so delightful to tread as well? (RCM-7)

The universe is nothing but Braham-Rāma who has become evolved into so many different forms—with each form being but a wave in that Ocean. The Jnāna-Yogi's method is to negate all the worldly waves of the universe and thereby see just the underlying Ocean of Rāma. Do note: the Bhakta-Yogi too is questing after the same underlying Ocean but he doesn't negate the waves—that being too difficult an undertaking—instead he catches hold of one beauteous wave and embraces it as being fully representing the Ocean: his Lord-God.

53 Bhakti-Yoga

The path of Bhakti-Yoga is in truth is the same quest for Braham as that of Jnāna-Yoga—except that the Bhakta picks one beautiful wave of that infinite Ocean to become the object of his Love. Aye, Love. The one prominent characteristics of Bhakti is Love, Love, Love—it is a path that begins with Love, continues in Love and ends in unending Love—when Braham, the ocean of love and bliss comes within reach. The Bhakta says:

Let others adore Braham, the primal existence,
the un-embodied formless supreme,
whom the Vedas hymn in endless verses;
as for me, my desire is just for Sita-Rāma—
the embodied and visible;
I turn for solacement just to Sita- Rāma,
whose love and grace remains causeless—
even unto the undeserving, poor, wretched, lowly.

O Lord, recognize me as thy servant and grant me just only Bhakti for thee; may thou ever abide in my heart. Of paradise and earthly pleasures I seek nothing. O Lord-God Sītā-Rāma, there is no other desire in my heart, I speak the truth and you know all my inmost thoughts: I Pray, please grant me only the intense-most devotion to thy holy feet, and make my heart clean of lust and of every other sin. O Lord, grant me just this boon: the blessing of constant devotion to thy lotus feet.

When one reaches the culmination of Bhakti—or rather, when the lower Gaun Bhakti ripens into the highest Parā-Bhakti—then every single moment when we are in that lofty state, we find ourselves abiding in Lord-God Rāma—who is existence-consciousness-bliss absolute.

Parā-Bhakti is intense love for Sītā-Rāma—extreme and indescribable—a state which has similitude to the Samādhi of Rāja-Yoga: a complete beatitude. Having gotten there, a person becomes one within Bliss and becomes mute remaining forever satisfied—there being nothing else to quest for, for he has reached the Ocean of Bliss itself.

This highest love of Bhakti cannot be reduced to any earthly benefit. When earthly benefits are sought in return for loving and venerating Sītā-Rāma—that is a very low state—somewhat like trading, a tit for tat, with very little of fidelity, somewhat like human love.

Unfortunately most people are like that, although they call themselves Bhaktas, but their devotion is not towards God but for their wishes, wants, desires, miracles. Completely infidel, whosoever promises them instant miracles, these people immediately abandon whosoever they may have been worshipping and gravitate instead to their new found "god", lining up outside this freshly minted so-called miracle-maker; and thus you will find Zindoos queued up even outside Zizlamist dhargas—places where Zindoo cows, who Zindoos ostensibly venerate, were once slaughtered in order to desecrate that place—which was once a Zindoo temple. Instead of being outraged, Zindoos now go to those very places to throw their money because through the propaganda machinery of movies and TVs—all in control of forces inimical to Sanātana-Dharma—the masses have been convinced that their wishes will become fulfilled there.

O fools, if you have to have miracles in your life, then Ekam-Sanātana-Dharma teaches us that we do not have to cower for help to the outside because we ourselves are the miracle-makers. Take to the path of Rāja-Yoga which is far speedier and you will get great powers—in fact when you reach the acme of perfection in any of the Yogic-paths you yourself become a powerhouse who can wreak miracles in anyone's life. Don't be going running after these true or fake miracle-makers, guruz, charlatans who may be after your money.

So that then is the danger of Bhakti—people becoming reduced to cowering herds visiting sham thatrī-barā cross-wielding priestz, miracle-makers, magicians, zizlamist pīr, fakir, graves, fake guruz—remaining slaves to their own wishes and wants rather than questing after the Truth, their true Self, Ātmā, Param-Ātmā, God, Sītā-Rāma. Unfortunately a majority of people pursuing their so called "Bhakti" path fall in this category, so be cautioned that Bhakti is a path where you can easily go astray, and instead of reaching bliss and freedom—one's goal in life—become instead degenerate slaves—the very opposite of that.

That is why the wisdom—which is innate to Jnāna—is very important in Bhakti as well. Without Jnāna, a Bhakta will likely walk into pitfalls where he will remain trapped throughout life. So although Bhakti is a very easy path, be sure to tread it with caution, with the light of Jnāna always by your side.

In Bhakti there should be no trade, no performing something to gain some earthly benefits—it should be performed only as the means for Self-realization and gaining nearness to our Lord-God—and that alone is true Bhakti.

So long as our worldly desires persist, true Bhakti has not yet entered into our hearts and in all likelihood we will end up becoming depraved slaves to our wants and desires—getting further entangled in the world—instead of walking towards freedom and its ensuant bliss.

The path of Bhakti-Yoga in its pristine form—desiring just only God, bereft of wants, wishes, desires for anything worldly—is found to be greater than the path of Karma-Yoga, and greater than Rāja-Yoga, and greater than Jnāna-Yoga—only by dint of the fact that it is very easy and replete with bliss from day one. These other paths have bliss as the objective—with the initial struggle remaining harsh and arduous—whereas Bhakti has bliss inbuilt into the very path itself. Bhakti is its own fruition, its own means, and its own end—because Bhakti itself is Bliss. So if you can manage to guard yourself against following its degenerate form—where you are venerating your own desires and wants rather than God—then Bhakti is the greatest path to endless bliss.

Bhakti is arrant devotion—an intense longing to become united with our source, our origin, becoming one with the Supreme-Self—with all the defilements upon the Self removed. Bhakti-Yoga is for one who is an emotional type—essentially a lover at heart—but who, having found no fidelity existing in human love, turns his face now towards a higher being who can reciprocate back his love and loyalty fully—and yes, that can only be Sītā-Rāma, and not any human.

The Bhakta is found loving and worshipping Lord-God Shri Sītā-Rāma with all the worldly methods at his disposal—using all sorts of rites, rituals, images, lamp, incense, recitations, lores, verses, chants, dresses, flowers, vows, fasts, festivities etc. However there is also a higher state—a supreme devotion called Parā Bhakti—where all these performances centered around forms, names, symbols, rituals, simply fall away unnoticed—naturally, on their own. Because now He whom you seek is right there before you.

Please note that in Bhakti we are questing after the same Braham—the formless ocean of consciousness—but we are venerating Him as Sītā-Rāma, God with form—because that makes our worship infinitely easier. It is rather difficult to love and venerate a God who has no form or name, so the Bhakta is just making his path that much easier when he uses an image to be the object of his veneration.

For a devotee, the unborn Braham—beyond the reach of mind and senses, without a beginning and end, the invisible, the indivisible—has become tangible: as Sītā-Rāma, the incarnate merciful God of immeasurable beauty, the mighty-armed Lord, the ornament of earth, the dispeller of all life's fears and sorrows.

Aye, unto Braham—who has created this vast fantastic creation in which everything is possible—is it then not possible that He, the formless, bodiless goes on to become the embodied Lord-God who is the creator of beings and things, of profound wisdom, the sustainer of life, the annihilator of

Māyā and her delusions, who brings everlasting delight to His devotees that chant His name?

Aye, verily He, whom the Vedic hymns venerate as Braham, the all-pervading supreme spirit, the unbegotten, the inaccessible, un-approachable, aloof; He whom ascetics manage to behold only when they have laboriously subdued their mind and senses; whom the virtuous attain after endless contemplation, penance and abstractions—for the devotees that very formless Braham becomes manifest on earth as the all-merciful Lord-God Shri Sītā-Rāma, the Lord of the three spheres, the all-radiant, unfailing benefactor, the destroyer of lust and all wickedness, the terminator of birth-death cycle—He who is fully accessible and brings delight to His devotees.

In the Lankā-Kānd of Rāmcharitmānas, the Rāmāyana of Tulsidāsa, we see Brahammā, the Creator of the world, making the following supplications unto Lord-God Shri Rāma, the human Avatāra of Mahā-Vishnu, after He has slain the demoniac monster Rāvana.

— ॐ —

जय राम सदा सुखधाम हरे । रघुनायक सायक चाप धरे ॥
jaya rāma sadā sukhadhāma hare, raghunāyaka sāyaka cāpa dhare.

भव बारन दारन सिंह प्रभो । गुन सागर नागर नाथ बिभो ॥
bhava bārana dārana siṁha prabho, guna sāgara nāgara nātha bibho.

तन काम अनेक अनूप छबी । गुन गावत सिद्ध मुनींद्र कबी ॥
tana kāma aneka anūpa chabī, guna gāvata siddha munīṁdra kabī.

जसु पावन रावन नाग महा । खगनाथ जथा करि कोप गहा ॥
jasu pāvana rāvana nāga mahā, khaganātha jathā kari kopa gahā.

जन रंजन भंजन सोक भयं । गतक्रोध सदा प्रभु बोधमयं ॥
jana raṁjana bhaṁjana soka bhayaṁ, gatakrodha sadā prabhu bodhamayaṁ.

अवतार उदार अपार गुनं । महि भार बिभंजन ग्यानघनं ॥
avatāra udāra apāra gunaṁ, mahi bhāra bibhaṁjana gyānaghanaṁ.

अज ब्यापकमेकमनादि सदा । करुनाकर राम नमामि मुदा ॥
aja byāpakamekamanādi sadā, karunākara rāma namāmi mudā.

रघुबंस बिभूषन दूषन हा । कृत भूप बिभीषन दीन रहा ॥
raghubaṁsa bibhūṣana dūṣana hā, kṛta bhūpa bibhīṣana dīna rahā.

गुन ग्यान निधान अमान अजं । नित राम नमामि बिभुं बिरजं ॥
guna gyāna nidhāna amāna ajaṁ, nita rāma namāmi bibhuṁ birajaṁ.

भुजदंड प्रचंड प्रताप बलं । खल बृंद निकंद महा कुसलं ॥
bhujadaṁḍa pracaṁḍa pratāpa balaṁ, khala bṛṁda nikaṁda mahā kusalaṁ.
बिनु कारन दीन दयाल हितं । छबि धाम नमामि रमा सहितं ॥
binu kārana dīna dayāla hitaṁ, chabi dhāma namāmi ramā sahitaṁ.
भव तारन कारन काज परं । मन संभव दारुन दोष हरं ॥
bhava tārana kārana kāja paraṁ, mana saṁbhava dāruna doṣa haraṁ.
सर चाप मनोहर त्रोन धरं । जलजारुन लोचन भूपबरं ॥
sara cāpa manohara trona dharaṁ, jalajāruna locana bhūpabaraṁ.
सुख मंदिर सुंदर श्रीरमनं । मद मार मुधा ममता समनं ॥
sukha maṁdira suṁdara śrīramanaṁ, mada māra mudhā mamatā samanaṁ.
अनवद्य अखंड न गोचर गो । सबरूप सदा सब होइ न गो ॥
anavadya akhaṁḍa na gocara go, sabarūpa sadā saba hoi na go.
इति बेद बदंति न दंतकथा । रबि आतप भिन्नमभिन्न जथा ॥
iti beda badaṁti na daṁtakathā, rabi ātapa bhinnamabhinna jathā.
कृतकृत्य बिभो सब बानर ए । निरखंति तवानन सादर ए ॥
kṛtakṛtya bibho saba bānara e, nirakhaṁti tavānana sādara e.
धिग जीवन देव सरीर हरे । तव भक्ति बिना भव भूलि परे ॥
dhiga jīvana deva sarīra hare, tava bhakti binā bhava bhūli pare.
अब दीनदयाल दया करिऐ । मति मोरि बिभेदकरी हरिऐ ॥
aba dīnadayāla dayā kariai, mati mori bibhedakarī hariai.
जेहि ते बिपरीत क्रिया करिऐ । दुख सो सुख मानि सुखी चरिऐ ॥
jehi te biparīta kriyā kariai, dukha so sukha māni sukhī cariai.
खल खंडन मंडन रम्य छमा । पद पंकज सेवित संभु उमा ॥
khala khaṁḍana maṁḍana ramya chamā, pada paṁkaja sevita saṁbhu umā.
नृप नायक दे बरदानमिदं । चरनांबुज प्रेम सदा सुभदं ॥
nṛpa nāyaka de baradānamidaṁ, caranāṁbuja prema sadā subhadaṁ.

— ॐ —

Glory to the Immortal-Lord: Rāma, who is Harī Vishnu the abode of Bliss, born as a prince in Raghu's lineage, wielding his bow and arrows; the lion-like Lord to rip in pieces the wild-elephant of troubles of a worldly-existence; He who is the ocean of perfection, the all-wise, the all-pervading Lord-God.

He in whose body is concentrated the incomparable beauty of a myriad Loves; whose virtues are sung endlessly by bards, saints, sages; O Hero of spotless renown who sanctifies all, who in His wrath didst seize Rāvan, as Garud might seize a monstrous serpent; O delight of mankind; dispeller of grief and fear; O Lord of supreme intelligence who ever abides beyond Māyā's passion; O Beneficent Incarnation of illimitable virtues and perfections—thou came to relieve the earth of her burdens, and to demonstrate what the embodiment of wisdom looks like.

Thou art the eternal all-pervading Braham, without a beginning, the One-Existence without a second—I fervently venerate thee, O Rāma, O fountain of mercy, O glory of the lineage of Raghu, who slew Dūshan and made a king of the ever faithful Vibhīshan. O storehouse of virtue and wisdom, everlasting, incomprehensible, beyond measure, unborn, all-pervading, pre-eminent in auspiciousness, beyond Māyā—I constantly adore thee, O Rāma, immense is the renown of thy glory and the supreme might of thy arms—deft in exterminating the hordes of the impious.

O friend and protector even of the undeserving suppliant—causeless thy grace—I worship thee, O perfection of beauty, along with Ramā thy consort. O destroyer of hideous sins of devotees, deliverer from the burden of birth-death cycle—thou art beyond the Māyā's ambit of cause and effects.

Armed with a mighty charming bow, quiver, arrows, O lotus-eyed Lord, paragon of sovereigns; abode of bliss, Lakshmī's glorious consort; the subduer of pride, lust, lying, and selfishness; thou art free of taints, irreproachable, imperishable, formless—imperceptible to the senses—yet present manifest in all forms, though of no determinate form; or as the Vedas have declared, like the light of the sun which is the same and yet visible variously as the various forms it lights upon—and aye, it is no mere quibble of speech.

O how fortunate, my Lord, are those—even these lowly Vānars—who are fortunate enough to be gazing reverently upon thy countenance; while accursed, O Harī, is that existence—even if it be immortal-gods like us of celestial spheres—which is lacking in devotion to thee and instead remains lost in sensual earthly pleasures.

Now, O Lord, as thou art compassionate to the suppliant, shower upon us gods thy grace; take away this deluding sentiency—by dint of which this universe appears differentiated from thee—which leads one to wrong actions deluded by Māyā, by dint of which one passes the days in merriments, mistaking the woes of the world to be the pleasures to go after.

Mercy, O mercy, O destroyer of the wicked, O beauteous jewel of the earth, He whose lotus feet are constantly cherished by Lord Shiva and Umā. O King of kings, Lord-God Shri Sītā-Rāma grant us just this boon: the blessing of a constant devotion to thy lotus feet which are the very perennial source of all blessings. (RCM-6)

KARMA-YOGA

Vidyā-putra Veni-prasād, a wandering sadhu from a kali-yuga of two billion years ago, is on a pilgrimage and has stopped at a village to rest. Here he is talking to people sitting under a banyan tree. Vidyā-putra said: "

When it comes to one's work-life, think of the woeful labor most people endure, the ignominy they submit to, the travails they undergo—because for most it's just a job to contend with, to somehow cope. But he who is fortunate enough to have embraced Ekam-Sanātana-Dharma, refuses to remain entrenched in this mindset—of a slave living through the grind of drudgery, or being exploited while staying demure and bedazed, or working like some donkey taking no delight in work—simply gaping expectantly and with delight on the carrots he will be fed when comes the payday—for he has taken to the path of Karma-Yoga instead.

— ॐ —

योगस्थः कुरु कर्माणि सङ्गं त्यक्त्वा धनञ्जय ।
yogasthaḥ kuru karmāṇi saṅgaṁ tyaktvā dhanañjaya
सिद्ध्यसिद्ध्योः समो भूत्वा समत्वं योग उच्यते ॥२-४८॥
siddhyasiddhyoḥ samo bhūtvā samatvaṁ yoga ucyate (BG-2-48)

Established in Yoga, perform Karma renouncing all attachments, O Dhananjaya, remaining unconcerned to the outcome—be it failure or success—this equanimity of mind is what is called Karma-Yoga.

— ॐ —

तस्मादसक्तः सततं कार्यं कर्म समाचर ।
tasmādasaktaḥ satataṁ kāryaṁ karma samācara
असक्तो ह्याचरन्कर्म परमाप्नोति पूरुषः ॥३-१९॥
asakto hyācarankarma paramāpnoti pūruṣaḥ (BG-3-19)

Remaining unattached, always perform your prescribed duties—remaining engaged in your Dharma. Verily a man attains the Supreme by performing unattached those Karma duties which are ordained to be performed.

If our Varna-Āshram and circumstances dictate that we should live in the world doing worldly chores remaining fully trenched within the world—which is the case with most of us—then we necessarily have take to the path of Karma-Yoga, the Pravritti-Mārg of Sanātana-Dharma. This way we not only retain our peace of mind but going way, way beyond that, we are actually able to attain to the state of totality of bliss and emancipation.

Karma-Yoga exhorts: Join yourself to work but without binding yourself down to the task—remaining detached. It says: Join just only to the cause of work—without joining to the desires and payoffs which usually persist inherent in tasks. It advices: Remain attached to work and yet stay detached to the fruits thereof—looking expectantly for nothing in return. Consider it just as my duty done; period.

— ॐ —

यस्त्विन्द्रियाणि मनसा नियम्यारभतेऽर्जुन ।
yastvindriyāṇi manasā niyamyārabhate'rjuna
कर्मेन्द्रियैः कर्मयोगमसक्तः स विशिष्यते ॥ ३-७॥
karmendriyaiḥ karmayogamasaktaḥ sa viśiṣyate (BG-3-7)

One who knows rightly—and consequently excels—is one who performs Karma-Yoga with the organs of actions outwardly while simultaneously remaining unattached within, with his sense-organs remaining within the control of his mind all the time.

Karma-Yoga leads to knowledge of the within Self which is replete with bliss, which knowledge in turn leads to emancipation—a complete freedom from the bonds of repeated births and deaths. Remember: although questing for self-realization, the Karma-Yogi—unlike the Jnāna-Yogi—does not shy from work. Because to give up work which is calling to be done—that which is our call of duty—will only lead to misery and hell, not just within our mind but all around: within our life, family and society as well.

In the Bhagavad-Gītā we see how Arjuna is shirking from the battle that stands confronting him; he is running away from his obligated duties as a householder and a Kshatriya. Then Lord Krishna exhorts: Rise up and fight O Arjuna; for fortunate is the Kshatriya who gets to fight in a battle that has thus come unsought. It is verily an open portal to heaven when your obligated duties stand before you demanding you perform them.

— ॐ —

अथ चेत्त्वमिमं धर्म्यं सङ्ग्रामं न करिष्यसि ।
atha cettvamimaṁ dharmyaṁ saṅgrāmaṁ na kariṣyasi
ततः स्वधर्मं कीर्तिं च हित्वा पापमवाप्स्यसि ॥२-३३॥
tataḥ svadharmaṁ kīrtiṁ ca hitvā pāpamavāpsyasi (2-33)

If you do not fight this righteous war, then shirking your duty and losing your reputation, you will incur sin as well.

In Karma-Yoga, work is performed for work's sake—for the sake of our Dharma, for discharging our obligated duties as called for by our situation within the Varna-Āshram system of Ekam-Sanātana-Dharma. Such duties—which are performed purely with the intention of doing our Dharma—bring on no bondages upon the Self.

— ॐ —

सुखदुःखे समे कृत्वा लाभालाभौ जयाजयौ ।
sukhaduḥkhe same kṛtvā lābhālābhau jayājayau
ततो युद्धाय युज्यस्व नैवं पापमवाप्स्यसि ॥२-३८॥
tato yuddhāya yujyasva naivaṁ pāpamavāpsyasi (BG-2-38)

Treating everything alike—regarding happiness and sorrow, gain and loss, victory and defeat, all to be equal—make yourself ready for the duty to battle; fighting this way, you will not incur sin.

— ॐ —

त्यक्त्वा कर्मफलासङ्गं नित्यतृप्तो निराश्रयः ।
tyaktvā karmaphalāsaṅgaṁ nityatṛpto nirāśrayaḥ
कर्मण्यभिप्रवृत्तोऽपि नैव किञ्चित्करोति सः ॥४-२०॥
karmaṇyabhipravṛtto'pi naiva kiñcitkaroti saḥ (4-20)

Giving up attachment to work and its fruit, ever content and without any recourse [except God]—such a one does not really do anything even though physically engaged in work.

And when no pleasures or desires or fear or pain return back to us from work done, then we soon get to that point where we can attain to our divinity in Infinite-Bliss—become one in Braham.

You will notice this one thing with the Karma-Yogi: that wherever he passes though, things begin to sparkle, and the ambience glows in the luster of his presence—with the world rendered brighter than before, becoming a better place. That is so because all the Yogi's Karmas are performed only in the cause of Ekam-Sanātana-Dharma—which has its origin in the divine being Braham—and not for any person; and that alone imparts him that sparkle, that luster.

The attitude of Karma-Yogi is:

I have come upon this earth for the work of Ekam-Sanātana-Dharma—it is what steers my life. I am guided by my Dharma, ever listening to my call of duty—work which has been appointed for me. Nay, I am not a slave to the world, but I am Sanātana-Dharma's vital pillar; and it is my service unto Dharma that makes me and my work divine; and I will perform all my obligated duties—whether good or bad, or coarse or fine.

Toiling day and night full of infinite zeal, I work in the cause of my Dharma, led by the floodlight of Sītā-Rāma and Sanātana-Dharma —that penetrating clear light that has guided humanity for ages and has never led the world astray.

Helps, betrayals, successes, failures—all that come my way, I gather them all together into a bundle of supreme-aloofness and then I submerge it all into the infinite depths of my Dharma, my God, my Sītā-Rāma.

— ॐ —

गतसङ्गस्य मुक्तस्य ज्ञानावस्थितचेतसः ।
gatasaṅgasya muktasya jñānāvasthitacetasaḥ
यज्ञायाचरतः कर्म समग्रं प्रविलीयते ॥४-२३॥
yajñāyācarataḥ karma samagraṁ pravilīyate (BG-4-23)

Free of attachments, with no identification with the body, with his intellect established in wisdom, he whose works are performed only as a Yajna unto the Lord-God—all his Karmas entirely melt away from him.

Struggling in the toils and blows related to work, I may at times be bruised and wounded, but only undergoing the mortification of Dharma I remain inured, endured, secured. In Dharma's penance, I may have to go hungry or diet just on grass, even lay down my life, but I will undergo all mortifications without even thinking of them to be such.

And when the time for me comes, I shall fold away all work—as one completely uninvolved, untroubled, aloof, detached. Aye, once upon a time I had received from my Dharma the charge of my duties; and my obligated Dharma now lies done—my toil and labor completed; and now I lay my body to rest at Sītā-Rāma's feet and now I let my Ātmā submerge into His Infinite-Light, never to again be reborn and return to earth.

Though a great warrior all throughout life, struggling, fighting tooth and nail, in all endeavors—but at the end of it all, a true Karma-Yogi just walks away unconcerned, having not made a single tie or attachment that will pull him back again into this sordid world of sorrowful existence.

RĀJA-YOGA

Vidyā-putra Veni-prasād, a wandering sadhu from a kali-yuga of two billion years ago, is on a pilgrimage and has stopped at a village to rest. Here he is talking to people sitting under a banyan tree. Vidyā-putra said: "

In life, at the very outset we have to realize that our Self—that from where our sense of "I" emanates—is not the body. We are not this body but are in fact of the nature of pure consciousness.

Even a little pondering and self-enquiry and a deep dive within, will lead us to the realization that we are not this external crust called the body but an awareness—a consciousness. The body parts can be severed without impacting the sense of wholeness of the "I"—which still remains intact. Most people will soon arrive at the realization that they are not this body but the mind. And with a little training in Rāja-Yoga they will further realize that we are not this mind either but its deeper essence: the Ātmā.

Sooner or later we have to wake up to the reality that we are in fact divine beings who have fallen from our pristine essence. This fall begins right from our birth—when the pristine Ātmā finds itself entrapped in the body and starts considering itself to be a mind, and with time we become further conditioned to continue abiding on the false side of our true nature; and by the time we grow up and realize what is going on, our awareness has already become firmly entrenched in the muck of Māyā and its ignorance—considering ourselves to be merely body and mind, a slave to pleasure giving sense-objects, alike pavlovian dogs—all the result of our mind become continually trained the wrong way our entire lives—until we manage to attain mental maturity and begin to question it all especially if we are fortunate enough to have Sanātana-Dharma in our life.

Yoga is the method of retraining the mind by cutting off this degenerate dependency on sense-objects to persist abiding as the continuing source of our happiness, and come by the realization that we ourselves are the ocean of blissful consciousness, needing nothing at all from the outside—which external in fact is a toxicity that is tainting our state of blissfulness.

We are not really this mind, with all its memories and thoughts which are all found evanescent—but something beyond, something that is abidingly lasting. As we discover in meditation, these memories and thoughts—the mind itself—can all be wiped off, severed away, lapse, but all that doesn't impact the sense of wholeness of the "I" which still remains intact despite any of those.

In fact the mind is simply a tainted state of our true pristine awareness—which pure state is extremely blissful, potent, replete with powers, and that pristine awareness is called the Ātmā: a pure never dying existence repleteful of blissful consciousness. And Rāja-Yoga is the discipline which teaches how to attain this state of immaculate awareness called the Ātmā.

The Ātmā is the witness, the seer—pristine consciousness at its essence, and its reaction to the externals is what we call the mind. When that pure consciousness becomes tainted with cognizance of the external, it remains identified with that modified state—losing sense of its seminal pristine essence.

— ॐ —

योगश्चित्तवृत्तिनिरोधः ॥१.२॥

yogaścittavṛttinirodhaḥ (YS-1.2)

— ॐ —

Yoga is restraining the pristine state of Chitta (our awareness) from becoming deformed, from taking on various forms.

Rāja-Yoga is all about restraining our innate consciousness from taking various modifications so that it abides in its own unsullied, pristine unmodified state—as pure consciousness. The restraining of consciousness from becoming tainted, though difficult, is attainable and made possible through practice.

Success in Yoga comes by first developing detachment—exercising control over the mind and sense-organs, restraining them away from sense-objects; and then further through practice—which is a continuous struggle to keep the mind and sense-organs perfectly restrained. There are several Yama and Niyama—the Do's and Dont's of Yoga—that help us develop detachment and make the control upon our minds steady and firm.

Normally our cognition of things—which comprises of the seer, seen and the act of seeing—all remain jumbled as one. But the Yogi is able to make his awareness fine and finer until he is able to discern each of them separately, and further is able to hold on to any of the aspect of awareness he chooses to stay at.

The practice of Yoga goes through several succeeding stages of meditation: from deliberating upon many, the mind is trained to becomes intent upon one object; then eliminating the outer gross form of the object, one learns to concentrate upon its subtle form; then eliminating even the subtle form, one reflects just on the essence of the object; then eventually when even that is eliminated, the mind remains simply as a witness, a seer that views nothing—a reflector shining all aglow, but actually reflecting upon nothing.

At this point the seen completely disappears and only the Seer remains; the Chitta becomes merged in its own essence, with all awareness of the external gone. That is Samādhi where just the sense of pristine "I" remains. But there is even a higher stage called Nirvikala Samādhi where even that sense of self and time melts, everything vanishes away. One becomes One in Braham then; and that is the ultimate aim of Rāja-Yoga.

— ॐ —

यत्रोपरमते चित्तं निरुद्धं योगसेवया ।
yatroparamate cittaṁ niruddhaṁ yogasevayā
यत्र चैवात्मनात्मानं पश्यन्नात्मनि तुष्यति ॥६-२०॥
yatra caivātmanātmānaṁ paśyannātmani tuṣyati (BG-6-20)

सुखमात्यन्तिकं यत्तद् बुद्धिग्राह्यमतीन्द्रियम् ।
sukhamātyantikaṁ yattad buddhigrāhyamatīndriyam
वेत्ति यत्र न चैवायं स्थितश्चलति तत्त्वतः ॥६-२१॥
vetti yatra na caivāyaṁ sthitaścalati tattvataḥ (BG-6-21)
यं लब्ध्वा चापरं लाभं मन्यते नाधिकं ततः ।
yaṁ labdhvā cāparaṁ lābhaṁ manyate nādhikaṁ tataḥ
यस्मिन्स्थितो न दुःखेन गुरुणापि विचाल्यते ॥६-२२॥
yasminsthito na duḥkhena guruṇāpi vicālyate (BG-6-22)
तं विद्याद् दुःखसंयोगवियोगं योगसंज्ञितम् ।
taṁ vidyād duḥkhasaṁyogaviyogaṁ yogasaṁjñitam
स निश्चयेन योक्तव्यो योगोऽनिर्विण्णचेतसा ॥६-२३॥
sa niścayena yoktavyo yogo'nirviṇṇacetasā (BG-6-23)

That state—in which the mind subdued through the practice of Yoga becomes completely settled, in which the self rejoices only in the Self by a mind purified through reasoning; that state—in which one realizes the absolute, transcendent bliss experienced via pure intellect; established in which state one never wavers from the Truth; that state—attaining which one discovers no other acquisition which could be greater than that; established in which state one is not moved even by the heaviest of sorrows—verily that state is designated as Yoga—untouched by any contact with pain. That Yoga should be practiced resolutely, unwearied in spirit.

Now a days Yoga remains mostly identified with physical exercises; but this physical aspect of Yoga—called the Hatha-Yoga—doesn't gain you real abiding happiness. By contrast Rāja-Yoga at its essence is primarily about our inner world rather than the external. It is a discipline by which one makes one's awareness—which otherwise remains weighed down with distractions and restlessness—to become concentrated and one-pointed, eventually leading one to a state of complete beatitude called Samādhi.

— ॐ —

वितर्कविचारानन्दास्मितारूपानुगमात् संप्रज्ञातः ॥१.१७॥
vitarkavicārānandāsmitārūpānugamāt saṁprajñātaḥ (1.17)

— ॐ —

Samprajnāta (trance-with-cognition) is accompanied with vitarka (reasoning, philosophical curiosity), vichār (meditative thought), ānanda (elation) and asmitā (sense of this-I-am, or ego).

Mental fluctuations is merely the Seer shining inwardly and also outwardly on things. Once it stops reflecting upon the outside objects and remains fully focused dwelling just only on the within, then a mental cessation ensues—the mind begins to quell down, vanish. By a continual practice of this notion of cessation, the mind—having no object to grasp—starts becoming as if it were non-existent.

It is as if a resplendent crystal refuses to disperse its shine upon the outside and only remains self-resplendent within, not letting its rays to disperse to the outside. At that time the entire apparatus of the mind-stuff becomes suspended. The mind with all its faculties begins to merge into its innate essence; it can be said to have died, remaining only as pristine Intelligence with the potential to know anything but actually reflecting no knowledge—remaining just as itself, choosing to know nothing but itself.

Thus through Yoga, overpowering the prototypic fluctuating agitated state of mind that remains obsessed with sense-objects, the Yogi has gradually brought it to the state of staying untainted, silent, unmarred—remaining focussed and pointed upon just one: itself.

And eventually the Yogi merges even that final wave, called the ego, into its very essence: the Ātmā; and now he abides completely unwavering—like a flickerless flame.

— ॐ —

यदा विनियतं चित्तमात्मन्येवावतिष्ठते ।
yadā viniyataṁ cittamātmanyevāvatiṣṭhate
निःस्पृहः सर्वकामेभ्यो युक्त इत्युच्यते तदा ॥६-१८॥
niḥspṛhaḥ sarvakāmebhyo yukta ityucyate tadā (BG-6-18)
यथा दीपो निवातस्थो नेङ्गते सोपमा स्मृता ।
yathā dīpo nivātastho neṅgate sopamā smṛtā
योगिनो यतचित्तस्य युञ्जतो योगमात्मनः ॥६-१९॥
yogino yatacittasya yuñjato yogamātmanaḥ (BG-6-19)

Thoroughly purged of the cravings for sense-enjoyments, when the disciplined mind gets firmly riveted upon the Self alone, then that person is said to be established in Yoga. The controlled mind of a Yogī who is practicing meditation on the Self, has its perfect epitome in the flame of a lamp—placed in a windless place—which does not flicker.

The restriction of all mental fluctuations—which are hindrances in our realizing our true nature—is the sole goal of Rāja-Yoga. By its practices all hindrances disappear. The begrimed crust—called the mind—which has become accumulated upon our awareness, under which's thraldom our true awareness—of the Ātmā—has become confined, that now becomes completely loosened through Yoga and is eventually rent asunder. The mind essentially dies with all its waves, fluctuations, thoughts having disappeared.

Then one's awareness comes by its true essence—existence, consciousness, bliss absolute. Who we truly are becomes actually realized when our mind has become dissolved in the act of Yoga called Nirvikalpa Samādhi—a complete beatitude.

— ॐ —

श्रुतिविप्रतिपन्ना ते यदा स्थास्यति निश्चला ।
śrutivipratipannā te yadā sthāsyati niścalā
समाधावचला बुद्धिस्तदा योगमवाप्स्यसि ॥२-५३॥
samādhāvacalā buddhistadā yogamavāpsyasi (BG-2-53)

When your understanding, now perplexed by variegated hearing, has gone past that—to rest in Samādhi, unwavering and steady—then you shall have attained to perfection in Yoga.

JNĀNA-YOGA

Vidyā-putra Veni-prasād, a wandering sadhu from a kali-yuga of two billion years ago, is on a pilgrimage and has stopped at a village to rest. Here he is talking to people sitting under a banyan tree. Vidyā-putra said: "

We are the Ātmā—purely a consciousness, beyond the ambit of the physical. In actuality, at our very essence, we truly are That-One-Existence-Braham which the sword cannot pierce, which the water cannot meld, which the air cannot dry, which the fire cannot burn, which cannot be held confined in space—we dwell completely beyond the reach of the five elements and the five senses.

Unfortunately we humans mostly live abiding in amnesia, remaining forgetful of who we are, but truly, truly, truly, we are just the Ātmā which exists rooted in Braham—also called God.

— ॐ —

नैनं छिन्दन्ति शस्त्राणि नैनं दहति पावकः ।
nainaṁ chindanti śastrāṇi nainaṁ dahati pāvakaḥ
न चैनं क्लेदयन्त्यापो न शोषयति मारुतः ॥२-२३॥
na cainaṁ kledayantyāpo na śoṣayati mārutaḥ (BG-2-23)

Weapons do not cut the Ātmā; and fires burn It not; and water cannot drench It; nor can It the winds dry.

Verily, we are the Ātmā in Braham, the holy one, perfect and pure, free and unbound, but by dint of our wrong conditioning—not just from this birth but over the eons—we have come to think ourselves to be a mind, and the senses, and we have become hopelessly tied to this body—in-fact thinking ourselves to be nothing but a body; this is Māyā which deludes the beings of the world.

— ॐ —

नादत्ते कस्यचित्पापं न चैव सुकृतं विभुः ।
nādatte kasyacitpāpaṁ na caiva sukṛtaṁ vibhuḥ
अज्ञानेनावृतं ज्ञानं तेन मुह्यन्ति जन्तवः ॥५-१५॥
ajñānenāvṛtaṁ jñānaṁ tena muhyanti jantavaḥ (BG-5-15)

Braham—present everywhere and in all, same to all, partial to none—is never really involved with the virtues, sins, declension of beings; but because Truth of the Ātmā remains clouded in Ignorance, the embodied beings of the world persist degraded and bewildered, by dint of delusions.

It is Rāma's Māyā which has spun out this deluding universe in which we—who are the Ātmā—roam around persisting befuddled, thinking ourselves to be a lowly Jiva, a slave to all and sundry. Ignorance of our true nature leads to bondage which produces misery. The way out of misery is to get out of the clutches of Māyā by knowing who we are, and the direct path to that is the path of Jnāna-Yoga.

Jnāna comprises of eliminating our Ignorance, to recondition our awareness back to naught—its pristine state; to arrive at our essence realizing that we are just the Ātmā rooted in Braham—nothing more, nothing less.

— ॐ —

ज्ञानेन तु तदज्ञानं येषां नाशितमात्मनः ।
jñānena tu tadajñānaṁ yeṣāṁ nāśitamātmanaḥ
तेषामादित्यवज्ज्ञानं प्रकाशयति तत्परम् ॥५-१६॥
teṣāmādityavajjñānaṁ prakāśayati tatparam (BG-5-16)

When Nescience is destroyed in the light of Jnāna—Knowledge of the Ātmā—then one's awareness, shining like the sun, reveals everything—right up to the Supreme-Being Braham.

Other than Jnāna—the knowledge whereby we realize who we truly are—there is no other way to complete emancipation. The other paths—Karma, Bhakti-Yoga—take us close to liberation, but to be actually freed, we have to step across the threshold of Jnāna averring: I negate all these waves, I reject everything—I just am the pristine consciousness Braham.

A Bhakta can reach his God, but for attaining emancipation forever—for the drop to merge back into the ocean—he must give up both God and himself and step across the portal of Jnāna declaring: there is no I, no you, no God, just only Braham, nothing less, nothing more, nothing else.

A Rāja-Yogi can arrive to the state of Samādhi but unless he reaches there having taken recourse to Jnāna he will return from there, and his mind will congeal back. But when he reaches Samādhi first having stepped across the portal of Jnāna—knowing that there is no I, no ego, no mind, just only Braham and nothing else—then, unless he wishes to return, he will not return and will merge in Braham, and his body will drop away from him.

So even having come by perfection in the other paths, one should strive for complete salvation by means of a complete embrace in Jnāna. We have been suffering in this worldly ocean of births and deaths in our long, long journey spanning the ages, and only Jnāna will take us completely out of this cycle—or else, even having attained perfection, upon death we shall dwell as beings in some high spheres, enjoying many pleasures there, but still remain bound and confined, never merging back into the ocean, never becoming infinite—verily God Himself.

For our complete liberation, this merely getting rid of our iron chains and reaching the golden state using the paths of Bhakti, Karma, Yoga, will not suffice; instead the wise erudite person eventually gives up even the golden chains which still bind him down—he gives up all works, even the good; all virtues, even the personal-God he loves—and this way he rents asunder all the bonds which have held him bound into this web of births and deaths for so long.

चित्तस्य शुद्धये कर्म न तु वस्तूपलब्धये ।
cittasya śuddhaye karma na tu vastūpalabdhaye ,
वस्तुसिद्धिर्विचारेण न किञ्चित्कर्मकोटिभिः ॥११॥
vastusiddhirvicāreṇa na kiñcitkarmakoṭibhiḥ (VCM-11)

On its own, work cannot impart Self-Realization (the attainment of oneness between the Ātmā and Braham). Work may lead to the purification of mind but never to the direct perception of Reality. Verily the attainment of Reality (Self-Realization) is brought about only through the act of Intellect—the discrimination of the Real from the non-Real—and not in the least by tens of millions of worldly actions.

However the path of pure Jnāna is quite hard, requiring one to renounce all possessions—because where there is unity and nothing else, then all sense of me and mine drops away naturally. Where it's all just I, all notions of possessions necessarily fade away—for other than I, what is there to crave or possess?

We cannot take up exclusively to the path of Jnāna-Yoga until we are ready to renounce everything— essentially give up on family and worldly life. This is called Pūrna-Vairāgya in Sanskrit, meaning Complete-Renunciation.

तद्वैराग्यं जिहासा या दर्शनश्रवणादिभिः ।
tadvairāgyaṁ jihāsā yā darśanaśravaṇādibhiḥ ,
देहादिब्रह्मपर्यन्ते ह्यनित्ये भोगवस्तुनि ॥२१॥
dehādibrahmaparyante hyanitye bhogavastuni (VCM-21)

Transient as they are, the desire to give up of all ephemeral delights of sense-objects—like sight, touch etc., that have their origin in the realm of the non-Real—ranging from the enjoyments derived through the body of mortals to that of king of gods—that is designated to be *Vairāgya*—Renunciation.

A Sanyāsi must take complete vow of Vairāgya—not just mentally but physically as well. However in preparation for that final Sanyāsa—which Sanātana-Dharma exhorts we all do in the final fourth stage of our life—we can make a beginning starting now itself, by adopting a mental attitude towards it—abiding as a Vairāgi in spirit, by staying detached from beings and things, by affirming that nothing or no one in this world is really mine.

Aye, we can still stand in Jnāna for support while treading the other paths, but to embrace it as the Yogic discipline to attain our oneness in Braham, would mean renouncing everything and abiding in the knowledge of complete non-duality in actuality, and not merely acknowledging it or giving it our mental assent. Most of us are not ready for that until we are old and can see death waiting for us yonder.

Sanātana-Dharma enjoins each and everyone of us—when we become old and can see death standing there on the horizon—to completely give up all worldly pursuits, give up on enjoyments and wealth, to leave all the cares of the world behind, and appoint a heir and start preparation for retirement, and then head towards the forests—and there at last fully embrace Pūrna Jnāna and Vairāgya: renounce everything and remain fully riveted around Sītā-Rāma, and realize our oneness in Him—which Sanātana-Dharma had been exhorting throughout our lives we do—but mandates that we do so at least now.

All the duties of the householder are but preparations towards this point in life, when all the bonds that bind the Ātmā to the world must be forever severed asunder. Sanyāsa Āshram is the fourth Āshram of the Sanātana-Dharma's Varna-Āshram system and when we reach there, we should renounce the world completely and devote the remainder of our life for self-realization, know of our Self to be the Ātmā rooted in the Param-Ātmā, the one-abiding-existence. Taking to Sanyāsa in the fourth quarter of our life, we should sever away all bonds that still bind us to the worldly life and completely abandon this thirsting after life and its pleasures—so that there will be no more births and deaths for us, so that we may finally escape from this vicious transmigratory cycle which is rife with sorrows, so that when we die, there are no more cravings nagging at us to return here once again donning another body.

The aim of Jnāna-Yoga is the same as that of Bhakti, Karma, Yoga but this path is rather distinctly stark and unique. Utilizing the power of intellect, this path is for the strong-minded and the rational rather than the emotional, or the devotional, or the battler, or the worker. This path is for the brave-heart who forges his path to the realization of the Self purely by himself and taking recourse just to his intellect.

For the Jnāna-Yogi there is none of our usual faiths and beliefs, no religious superstitions, dogmas, rites, rituals, no visiting temples or waving lights, even no sitting down in meditation to concentrate upon a point—because he is meditating on Braham all the time, non-stop, even with open eyes, even when talking, even when engaged in thought, with his mind just dwelling on Braham, negating all these visible waves and perceiving just only the tranquil ocean of consciousness Braham all the while, seeing Him alone behind everyone and everything.

The Jnāna-Yogi has no use of images and crosses—he has emptied his bag of all these long ago; for him there is no going to zhurches, zosques and listening to the same old, same old mindless babble; no bowing before any god or man or mullaz or priestz; no rotating his neck or going up and down on his knees muttering inanities; no favorite direction he must bow to, or a sacred day to demonstrate his allegiance to some odd god sitting in the sky, or a book he must learn his daily lessons from, to prove that he is a good boy to his teacher sitting in Shangri-la wielding a stick—nay, the Jnāna-Yogi is beyond all this kidishness and manipulations of humans going on in the name of religions.

The Jnāṇa-Yogi abides in complete freedom. Perceiving nothing else at all, he just sees only the consciousness of Braham pervading the entirety of the universe, and he realizes that he himself is that Braham whom the world is worshipping as God.

— ॐ —

अहो विकल्पितं विश्वमज्ञानान्मयि भासते ।
aho vikalpitaṁ viśvamajñānānmayi bhāsate ,
रूप्यं शुक्तौ फणी रज्जौ वारि सूर्यकरे यथा ॥२-९॥
rūpyaṁ śuktau phaṇī rajjau vāri sūryakare yathā (AG-2-9)

Aho!
This universe
—conceived in me, wrought out by Nescience—
is a seeming appearance
...alike the shells scattered on a beach
which are imagined to be silver due to greed;
...or alike a rope which becomes visible as snake,
from out of fear of darkness;
...or like the "water" of mirage seen to be real due to the deluding heat of desert.

— ॐ —

मत्तो विनिर्गतं विश्वं मय्येव लयमेष्यति ।
matto vinirgataṁ viśvaṁ mayyeva layameṣyati ,
मृदि कुम्भो जले वीचिः कनके कटकं यथा ॥२-१०॥
mṛdi kumbho jale vīciḥ kanake kaṭakaṁ yathā (AG-2-10)

All this here, emerges out of me;
it exists in me;
and within me again
it becomes dissolved
—like an earthen jar returning to its
component clay,
...or a wave
blending back into the water again,
...or a gold bracelet
melting into the pureness of its element
—having become bereft of form
bereft of name.

— ॐ —

अहो अहं नमो मह्यं विनाशो यस्य नास्ति मे ।
aho ahaṁ namo mahyaṁ vināśo yasya nāsti me ,
ब्रह्मादिस्तम्बपर्यन्तं जगन्नाशोऽपि तिष्ठतः ॥२-११॥
brahmādistambaparyantaṁ jagannāśo'pi tiṣṭhataḥ (AG-2-11)

Aho! How grand!
Salutations to 'me'—
of whom there is never any destruction—
who always abide undestroyed unaffected—
who endures unabated even after destruction of the last manifestation.

After the whole universe
—from the god Brahammā down to a tiny straw—
go vanishing without a trace,
'I', as the Ātmā,
still endure.

Vidyā-putra Veni-prasād, a wandering sadhu from a kali-yuga of two billion years ago, is on a pilgrimage and has stopped at a village to rest. Here he is talking to people sitting under a banyan tree. Vidyā-putra said: "

- The Section on Adharma -

Adharma: Just like the backdrop of Bhagavad-Gītā this world is an arena where the battle of Dharma and Adharma is continually playing out, but most times we remain blissfully aware of that. But it is a battle alright; and to be able to win the fight on behalf of Sanātana-Dharma we have to first know of our foemen. This Shatru-Bodh—becoming aware of the enemy—is the first step in being able to defeat it but most Zindoos lack this Shatru-Bodh entirely. Therefore it doesn't suffice to know just of Dharma but one must remain acutely cognizant of its polar reverse as well—Adharma that exists as a monster a hundred times larger in the shape of amalgamation of Tamas, Rajas, and demoniac propensities—so that we can identify that which we necessarily have to contend with at every turn in life. In this section on Adharma we will try to identify some forces and ideologies that are in a vicious unrelenting battle against Ekam-Sanātana-Dharma.

Remember if Dharma doesn't become the predominant force in society, then Adharma starts to prevail and society comes to ruin—as has been happening in recent centuries. The structures of Varna-Āshram and family, the vital component upon which rests the framework of society, is now crumbling—spreading grief all around. People live in misery but try finding happiness in pets, games, competition, increasing riches, buying things, rivality, entertainment, gossip, the frivolous, bizarre, thrills, appearing relevant by showing-off, doing circus-tricks, poking their noses into other's affairs, gaining joy off other's misery, reality shows, feeling good because others are more wretched than I; pretense at charity, having to constantly find people more pathetic than ourselves, etc.

Adharma, the enemy who is constantly in battle against goodness—and that enemy could well be our own mind, or more likely the aggregate of many external devious minds that have become congealed into the several evil systems become dominant in world today—is a persistent scourge that is seen devouring the souls of humans. These demonical systems and institutions of Adharma must be fought tooth and nail and defeated. At this moment in history though Adharma is winning in a big way and the goodness of Dharma is headed to extinction; this has to be reversed by bringing the fight to their doors irrespective of whatever; it is better to pay that cost today than a 100-x cost your grandchildren will eventually end up paying.

In the Gītā we find Arjuna struck with fear at the prospect of ensuing carnage and he lays down his arms and is prepared to live on alms rather than defend himself; but Lord Krishna exhorts him to give up cowardice and perform his duties and fight—or else Adharma will become prevalent in the world. Arjuna picks up his bow and slays his enemies—even his own relatives and gurus—in the cause of protecting Dharma and end the reign of Adharma on earth. Unfortunately we have strayed so far away from that ideal today; reason being that we have stopped studying our original scriptures and just gulp down whatever the fake-guruz with their nefarious agendas are feeding us. Most of these guruz are themselves Adharmika, selfish and cowards, or bought out by the opposition: Kālnemis. Cowardice is a sign of Adharma; and not protecting oneself is the biggest Adharma—unless an individual has taken the vow of Sanyāsa, which is rarely the case.

Zindoos of Zindia: The Zindoos of Zindia, although they deem themselves to be very righteous and god-fearing, are in fact some of the worst Adharmika people on earth—because man's very primal Dharma is to first be a man—protect his women, family, honor, traditions, culture, ideology, the symbols and things he loves and holds sacred—but Zindoo leaders has forgotten of that very essential Dharma these past two-three millenniums.

Each one of us—be it as individuals or be it as people, race, nations—have been assigned a role—our Dharma—to enact in Rāma's drama; and Sītā-Rāma loves it only when are performing our Dharma, that role, well. And man's very first and foremost Dharma is to fulfill the obligation and defense towards his own being and existence; towards his own immediate family which made his existence into the world possible; towards his own lineage painstakingly forged link by link across the millenniums that eventually culminated into his birth—and which continuity of the chain he is obligated to pass into the future by entering the Grahastha- Āshram system, ensuring that the culture and traditions of Sanātana-Dharma carry on into the future. Aye, our very first Dharma and obligation is to the defense of Sanātana-Dharma and her Varna-Āshram system that made us possible and everything else comes next. If we cannot work in defense of our primal obligations, then of what avail anything else?

What avail money, career, success if you cannot protect your own culture and identity and end up rendered molded into a cuckoo-cookie, shaped by the Zenglishmen in their cookie-cutter mold they have exported all over the world, and which has just the Zenglishman's ideologies alone—their constitution, their systems, their judiciary, their religion, their philosophy, their sciences, their standards, their methods, their laws, their idea of good and evil, their idea of democracy—which's in-fact a Zizistianity inspired demon-cracy to control the world—their mannerisms, their idea of human rights, animal rights; their idea of soul and life, wrong and right. A monoculture of unproven ideology is being perpetrated by them giving it all they have got—like a virus their intent is to just taint the entire world with Zenglishness and Zizistianity/Zizlam; period. The beautiful world of yesteryears with all its diversities and charm has been shrunk into a village now, as they are so fond of claiming proudly—and of course it is a fully Zenglish village -- built around their zhurch/zosque -- with the entire earth looking the same now a days everywhere one goes.

By their self-arrogated prerogative which no other country dares to challenge, the Zenglish continue ruling the world by dint of momentum from their initial successes to stay as the basis for everything that must prevail on earth today—and which should be unhesitatingly accepted by all the races and nations; and they dictate to the world how to live, what to think, how to behave, how to act, what to watch etc.; and by dint of that they—who originally are from a land-size less than 0.3% of earth—rule over half the world. Building on the momentum of their successes—and which foundations rest on theirs savage conquests that are filled with the slush of human bodies, gore, massacres the world over—they continue to push upon humanity what are mostly half-baked untested ideas that have been in existence for just a couple centuries—which is peanuts -- and blood-soaked ones at that -- when it comes to the long human history of the tried and successful.

There's no telling what will be the eventual fallouts from their experimentation of selfishly pushing their imperialistic monoculture of mindless ideologies and religions down everyone's throats—but from Nature we know that Braham only loves diversity in all its hues when favoring life (compare earth to the monotonous dead mars for instance) and you better not be standing in Braham's way or a violent whiplash will follow. These selfish foolish beings, intent on pushing themselves upon everything and everyone on earth, might just end up converting our beautiful motleyed earth into a monotonic sight like the mars.

The anglosaxon elites—via Zamerica now—continuously use the two-sham religions and big corporations to make regime changes and wholesale export of their culture to extend their dominions and influences aggressively; and today over half the countries of the world are already their vassalages—not that those slavish people would ever admit to that; but a good way to identify slave-nations is the presence of foreign military bases on their soil; and/or the complete decimation of their age-old traditions and cultures—for example as has happened in Zindia, Zapan, Zorea… etc., a very long list of countries.

O world, it's still not too late; firmly rejecting these aggressive world-ruling Zenglish elites and these two demented religions of Zizistianity and Zizlam—with their crazed armies of bureaucrats, ceos, mullaz, priestz, pontiffz, fake-guruz that are madly pushing their imperialistic my-way-or-the-highway cultures, religions, ideologies etc.,—it is time for all self-respecting people to once again embrace their traditional cultures, yesteryear's life, life of simple joys, the customs and traditions of our ancestors, our original faiths—which have been derogatory labeled pagan/kafir by the Zizistians/Zizlamists. Imperialistic ideologies and religions must be completely eliminated from earth whatever the cost now, or else there will be no future for your grandchildren; because competing Imperialisms can only end with a BROB event given today's technology of nukes and bio-warfare.

Mind it, especially ye Zindoos: changing your ways and living like a worm that takes immediate detour upon meeting tiniest resistance; always compromising; altering your traditions, religion, customs under external pressures; cowering before everyone like cowardly slaves—just in order to survive as living breathing squirming worms, which ye Zindoos have been doing—is not man's Dharma and nor can it be called living. A lion will die but never change his ways and resort to eating grass and to bleat.

Lest it isn't already amply clear, let me explicitly clarify: Zindooism is the outer grungy crust of which Sanātana-Dharma is the crux. Sanātana-Dharma is to Zindooism as the Ātmā is to the Jiva—a once-upon-a-time purity and goodness which today has become dirty and begrimed, covered over with much dust and soot accumulated over time. Zindooism has to be cleaned of all its dirt and brought back to its pristine state of Ekam-Sanātana-Dharma, the glorious science of our grand Rishis.

The core of Sanātana-Dharma just emphasizes the Truth of Braham and the practical ways to attains one's oneness in Braham—reach that supreme Reality wherefrom we all once emerged. There is absolutely no centrical person, race, culture around which Sanātana-Dharma is woven—just only the Ultimate-Truth Braham. Sanātana-Dharma is not human-centric, race-centric, culture-centric and at one time all the ancient faiths were merely so many expressions of the central core of Sanātana-Dharma adapted to local cultures; and it is time all the races and nations fully reject the imperialistic madness of Zizistianity and Zizlam and come return to the traditions and religions of their ancestors.

Sanātana-Dharma is a glorious science and religion which exists independent of the bearers that happen to espouse it. Zindoos of Zindia just happen to be the current carriers of Sanātana-Dharma—and very poor examples of that now a days—and so never judge Sanātana-Dharma by merely looking at the present day Zindoo leaders of Zindia who are in fact a slur upon the glory of Sanātana-Dharma—and which shine Sītā-Rāma will likely pass to another nation and race in very near future if the Zindians do not mend their ways right away.

Lessons From Zhistory: We should always remain cognizant of our history and past mistakes and always be learning from it, staying alert. Unfortunately Zindoos have closed their history books and do not learn their lessons and consequently keep suffering. There is a saying, "Fool me once, shame on you; Fool me twice, shame on me." But not just twice, the Zindoos have been fooled and humiliated a million times but still refuse to respect themselves.

When it comes to bravery and pride, learn from Zamerica who might take a first hit but after that they learn such stern lessons from it and take such coercive steps that the enemy never dares raise its head ever again. Since 911 all entry points into Zamerica have posters of the burning twin towers and one simple message, "We Will Never Forget." A simple message, but most profound, which comes from the hearts of brave-men who did not make the first strike but ensured that it would be the last because the enemy was crushed into smithereens after that. The intelligent and brave do not need to be taught the same lesson over twice. Their two towers were destroyed and they destroyed two nations in revenge, and completely broke the terrorist organization that did it to them. Zapan hit them with pearl-harbor but Zamerica hit back with Hiroshima and Nagasaki—and made it a vassal state, completely destroying their culture—and consequently broke their spine. Zaddam had their President's face painted on the hallway for people to tread upon, and Zamerica destroyed Ziraq for that. A proud alive people never forget insults and injuries and always get back, and they first even-off the score before doing anything else. They understand that first and foremost you have to eliminate the threat to your existence—not that I am condoning the evil they brought to the world, but I admire their gallantry.

As part of world dominance which requires fooling the masses with empty rhetoric, Zamerica might mouth inanities about human-rights, democracy, goodness, freedom, blah, blah, which the world should adapt, but when it comes to their own self—on the inside Zamerica remains a proud military nation where none of that applies, where might alone rules, and they have firmly kept the politicians at bay from the real seats of power; and when it comes to their so-called 'democracy' of 'we-the-people'—a sham really since Zizistians and the elite's lackeys alone can occupy seats across all power-structures be it judiciary, executive, legislative, corporations, media/ internet-control—Zamerica, with their two-party-system, which's merely flavors around the same central core of sham/elites, are merely one-notch higher to the communist Zhina of the one-party-system; and when it comes to defending their own interests, especially when Zamerica gets riled and furious, then our blue-eyed white Uncle-Sam goes on a rampage pointing stern fingers at each and everyone of his enemy saying, "eff-you and you and you"—and they go ahead and do exactly that—screw them real good and then no one dares stand in the path of that enraged animal. Mind it I am not condoning mindless aggression—and Zamerica has done plenty of that and which must be berated—but their heroism which stands tall in the face of aggression has to be but admired, and it's just sad that they chose to build their life upon the 2000 year old fraud of Zizistianity instead of choosing the truth of Sanātana-Dharma—aye, intelligence is not really their forte, just only craftiness. Fully sensuous, they think just through their legs and biceps. Now contrast that to the Zindoos who have been getting butchered for centuries but still insist on embracing those very people and nations that massacred them by 100's of millions, still cowering before them like slaves. And this saddens Sītā-Rāma no end.

History has a tendency to repeats itself; and if not in this era, then perhaps in another Yuga or another Kalpa, you will find the same people, events, things cropping up on the world scene time and again—just as the same combinations of dice keep appearing given infinite time. So we will try to reproduce some zhistorical records from another Kali-Yuga in the hope that people of future Yugas will read and learn lessons from it. Most of it is paraphrased from what was available in public domain of those times when the events happened—in that Kali-Yuga billions of years ago.

The purpose of zhistory is to remind ourselves of past karmas and learn from that. Sanātana-Dharma has this Law-of-Karma which stipulates that no action goes in vain and we always end up reaping what we have sowed—be it good or bad. And this law is applicable not just to individuals but to people, races, nations; and not just the fruits of our individual karmas but we will also have to reap of our collective good/bad karmas, and it may sometimes take centuries or millenniums but eventually justice does get served by Nature. All the atrocities committed by materialistic nations pushing their ideology of mindlessly destroying the earth and her creatures the world over, all the countless creatures slaughtered in mass production factories, all the holocausts caused by sham religions upon the innocents etc., etc.,—each and every collective deed will get reconciled eventually. These collective sins might remain in abeyance for quite some time, but one day when their time comes they will strike back and demand a payback. Animal-slaughter will recoil as human-slaughter.

If we are part of the system that supported injustice without fighting against it, or at least raising our voices, then rest assured that we will end up having to pay for that collective sin. It is just that the reaction sometimes takes millenniums to arrive. For centuries now, the Himālayās have been rising a few inches every year as a result of tectonic plates in an ongoing collision, and once the plates begin to recoil from that collision, then there will be many fissures and earthquakes on earth—because for every action there is an inevitable reaction although the whole process may take millenniums to play out. And so for all the 100's of millions of Zindoos who have been massacred by the Zizlamists over the centuries, they will all get suitable justice in some future decade, century, millennium; have no doubts on that. We may forget and even forgive, but God will not; and He always has this justice which comes back to haunt the perpetrators—and it may even be a poetical justice sometimes—and the future generations of Zindoos could one day start respecting themselves and wake up to the genocide of their forefathers and will refuse to sleep until justice has been served and the souls of their ancestors can get to rest in peace eventually.

Eventually we all get to reap what we once sowed, and the balance does get restored. This is just the Law of Karma, plain and simple, so we have to be always very careful in making individual and collective choices in life. Why forget that were it not for Braham, we cannot even take our next breath, and we cannot control even a single cell of ostensibly "my body" to work the way we wish—let alone steer our whole body and life, or the destiny of millions upon earth the way the world-ruling elites and sham religions are doing as they go strutting around like cocks in their arrogance.

Today these uncivilized cannibals have been allowed to take control of the earth—I call them cannibals because a man who grows up sustained from the milk of a creature -- you being able to partake of cow's milk is because it's your own kind and nourishes you just as does your mother's milk -- and then later kill and eat that creature, is in irreverence of motherhood and everything civil, decent, fair, and tantamounts to cannibalism: eating the flesh of your own kind.

Alas, these uncivilized varlets are in power and they have nothing to offer but naked materialism and the bunk and sham of Zizistianity and Zizlam, which they are able to shove down the throats of illiterate and poor of Zindia, destroying age-old traditions, carrying out cultural genocide; arming communists, separatists, terrorists; destroying human lives, finding fault-lines, causing divisions, creating hatred, exporting their pestiferous culture, promoting lechery, pumping billions towards that and to pressure governments for policy changes to erode the last of that Zindian soil where Sanātana-Dharma can still take roots, spewing venom at those who resist—the Zenglishmen, Zizistians, Zizlamists are doing all that in Zindia just so they can fully destroy Sanātana-Dharma and harvest Zindoo souls to bring them to Zezus' and Zohmad's feet—their so called loving gods!—give me a break from this malefic poison on earth which treats humans like commodity, crop, flesh and blood to feast upon. God alone rules the world, O foolish ones, do not be getting too cocky. Braham is 100% in charge of the universe—not you or I or anybody. For now though Sītā-Rāma is just being kind and allowing humans a chance to redeem themselves and wake up from this madness and mend their ways even now. A BROB event (Big-Reset-of-Braham) is just waiting yonder on the horizon, just be mindful of that. Aye, you stand warned and this could as well be your warning straight from Sītā-Rāma.

These word might appear harsh to people of Zizistianity and Zizlam, but never forget how your very own forefathers were once converted—a long time ago they were made to choose between being converted or get killed; period. Whosoever you may be, once upon a time your ancestors were converted at the point of sword and made to adopt an evil creed void of goodness or substance and which you now serve—as you will find when you research your ancestry. I am still in Sanātana-Dharma because my forefathers did not convert but were likely killed; and I can fill many pages full of expletives but that wouldn't be mimicking even an infinitesimal part of what these two morbid sects did to Sanātana-Dharma and other faiths, and my harsh tones cannot compensate for even one innocent life lost at their hands—whereas as history shows, they slaughtered not one but over a billion innocents the world over and still continue with their macabre theme, albeit more subtly now, but still aggressively pushing their imperialistic ideology, and still walking the earth with impunity; all aglow and self-righteous, donning the garb of religion—and with the dullards of the world staying cowering before this evil instead of rising up to ban the morbid diseases plaguing humanity. —जय हनुमान ॐ जय सीताराम—

Lessons from Zhistory

Vidyā-putra Veni-prasād, a wandering sadhu from a kali-yuga of two billion years ago, is on a pilgrimage and has stopped at a village to rest. Here he is talking to people sitting under a banyan tree. Vidyā-putra said: "

Let us take some examples of the treatment of Zindoos by Zizlamic conquerors of Zindia from the written accounts of the Zizlamic historians themselves.

Shahab-ud-Din, King of Ghazni, the virtual founder of the Zizlamic Empire in Zindia (reign 1170-1206), put Prithwi-Raj, the King of Ajmer and Dihli, to death in cold blood. He massacred thousands of the inhabitants of Ajmer who had opposed him, reserving the remainder for slavery. After his victory over the King of Banaras the slaughter of the Zindoos is described as immense. None were spared except women and children who were taken in as slaves, and the carnage of the men was carried on until, as it has been said, the earth grew weary of the monotony.

Incidentally Shahab-ud-Din remains a very popular name amongst the Zizlamist converts of Zindia—the idea being to remind the Zindoos of the atrocities upon their ancestors and that too by thumbing their nose and rubbing it into their face, since they know that the Zindoo will just take it lying down, remaining ever mild, timid, stupid, his neck buried in the sand, ignorant of the genocide upon the Zindoos—past, present, or just waiting on the horizon mouth open.

In the Taj-ul-Mcfasir by Hasan Nizam-i-Naishapuri it is stated that when Qutab-ud-Din Aibak (reign 1194-1210) conquered Merath he demolished all the Zindoo temples of the city and erected mosques on their sites. In the city of Koil, now Aligarh, he converted Zindoo inhabitants to Zizlam by the sword and beheaded all who adhered to their religion. In the city of Kalinjar he destroyed one hundred and thirteen Zindoo temples, built mosques on their sites, massacred over one hundred thousand Zindoos, and made slaves of about fifty thousand more. It is said the place became black as pitch with the decomposing bodies of the Zindoos.

Incidentally the Zindoos are so large hearted that mosque and minaret—built after demolishing ancient Zindoo temples in Dihli—still stand proudly bearing the name of that tyrant Qutab. Adjacent to it also is a historical iron pillar there from Chandragupta times that doesn't rust—showcasing the advanced metallurgy that existed in Zindia thousands of years ago, and which pillar the Zizlamists tried to destroy but couldn't.

In the Tabaqat-i-Nasiri by Minhaj- ul-Siraj it is stated that when Muhammad Bakhtyar Khilji conquered Bihar he put to the sword about one hundred thousand Brahmins, and burnt a valuable library of ancient Sanskrit works.

Abdulla Wassaf writes in his Tazjiyat-ul-Amsar wa Tajriyat ul Asar that when Ala-ud-Din Khilji (reign 1295-1316) captured the city of Kambayat at the head of the gulf of Cambay, he killed the adult male Zindoo inhabitants for the glory of Zizlam, set flowing rivers of blood, sent the women of the country, with all their gold, silver, and jewels, to his own home, and made about twenty thousand maidens his private slaves.

Ala-ud-Din once asked his qazi what was the Zizlamic law prescribed for Zindoos. The qazi replied, "Zindoos are like dirt; if silver is demanded from them, they ought with the greatest humility to offer gold instead. And if a Zizlamic desire to spit into a Zindoo's mouth, the Zindoo should open it wide for that purpose. God created Zindoos to be slaves of the Zizlamists. The Prophet hath ordained that, if the Zindoos do not accept Zizlam, they should be imprisoned, tortured, and finally put to death, and their property confiscated." At this the monarch smiled and said he had not been waiting for an interpretation of the sacred law. He had already issued an order that everything be taken away from Zindoos leaving them just corn and coarse clothes sufficient to last for six months.

During Ala-ud-Din's reign men formerly in easy circumstances were reduced to beggary, and their wives obliged to resort to menial labor for their maintenance. In front of his palace the corpses of forty or fifty Zindoos were routinely present—killed that day for petty offences. Zindoos were punished with merciless severity for the most trifling offences. Ala-ud-Din Khilji was so cruel that he had his own brother and nephew flayed alive on the mere suspicion of disloyalty. He then had their flesh cooked and forced their children to eat it. What remained after the repast was thrown to the elephants to trample on.

Amir Khusrau writes in his Tawarikh Alai or Khazain- ul-Futuh that when the Emperor Firoz Shah Tughlak (1351-1388) took the city of Bhilsa in Bhopal, he destroyed all its Zindoo temples, took away their idols, placed them in front of his fort, and had them daily bathed with the blood of a thousand Zindoos. Tughlak twice plundered the country of Malwa, and took away everything he could find except earthen pots.

Today many places and roads in Zindia still proudly bear the name Tughlak, and those Zindoos—whose forefathers were butchered and their idols bathed with blood of their forefathers—merrily go driving to their office in their BMWs on Tughlak Road in Dihli, the very heart of Zindia, to make even more money—because you see for Zindoo elites money alone is everything, honor and self-respect be damned.

Jahangir's grandson the Emperor Aurangzeb was brought up a very strict Zizlamist. The following, according to the Mirat-i-Alam of the historian Bakhtawar Khan, shows how he treated Zindoos and their temples for the honor and glory of God and the success of what he considered the only true religion: 'Zindoo writers have been entirely excluded from holding public offices; and all the worshipping places of the infidels, and the great temples of these infamous people have been thrown down and destroyed in a manner which excites astonishment at the successful completion of so arduous an undertaking.'

The following is from the Maasir-i-Alamgiri: 'It reached the ears of His Majesty, the Protector of the Faith, that in the provinces of Thatha, Multan, and Banaras, but especially in the latter, foolish Brahmins were in the habit of expounding frivolous books in their schools, and that students, learned Zizlamists as well as Zindoos, went there even from long distances, led by a desire to become acquainted with the wicked sciences there taught. The Director of the Faith consequently issued orders to all the governors of provinces to destroy with willing hands the temples and schools of the infidels, and to put an entire stop to the teaching and practice of idolatrous forms of worship. It was subsequently reported to his religious Majesty, leader of the Unitarians, that in obedience to his orders, the Government officers had destroyed the temple of Vishwanath at Banaras. In the thirteenth year of Aurangzeb's reign this justice-loving monarch, the constant enemy of tyrants, commanded the destruction of the Zindoo temple of Mathura, and soon that stronghold of falsehood and den of iniquity was leveled with the ground. On its site was laid at great expense the foundation of a vast mosque.'

The Zizlamic historian thus describes the treatment of Satnamis by the Emperor Aurangzeb : 'A body of bloody miserable rebels, goldsmiths, carpenters, sweepers, tanners, and other ignoble beings, braggarts and fools of all descriptions became so puffed up with vain glory as to cast themselves headlong into the pit of destruction. Aurangzeb sent an army to exterminate and destroy these unbelievers. The heroes of Zizlam charged with impetuosity and crimsoned their sabres with the blood of these desperate men. The struggle was terrible. At length the Satnamis broke and fled, but were pursued with great slaughter.

'General Khan Jahan Bahadur arrived from Jodhpur bringing with him several cartloads of idols taken from the Zindoo temples which had been razed to the ground. Most of these idols, when not made of gold, silver, brass, or copper, were adorned with precious stones. It was ordered that some of them should be cast away in out-offices and the remainder placed beneath the steps of the grand mosque to be trampled under foot. There they lay a long time until not a vestige of them was left.

'In 1680 Prince Muhammad Azam and Khan Jahan Bahadur obtained permission to visit Udaipur. Two other officers at the same time proceeded thither to effect the destruction of the temples of the idolaters, which are described as the wonders of the age, erected by the infidels to the ruin of their souls. Twenty Rajputs had resolved to die for their faith. One of them slew many of his assailants before receiving his death blow. Another followed and another until all had fallen. Many of the faithful also had been dispatched when the last of these fanatics had gone to hell.

'Soon after Aurangzeb himself visited the Rana's lake and ordered all its temples to be leveled with the ground. Hasan Ali Khan then made his appearance with twenty camels taken from the Rana, and reported that the temple near the palace and one hundred and twenty-two more in the neighboring districts had been destroyed. He was rewarded by the emperor with the title of Bahadur.

'When Aurangzeb went to Chitaur, still one of the most beautiful of all ancient cities, he caused sixty-three temples there to be demolished. The Rana had now been driven forth from his country and his home, the victorious Ghazis had struck many a blow, and the heroes of Zizlam had trampled under their chargers hoofs the land which this reptile of the forest and his predecessors had possessed for a thousand years.

'Abu Turab, who had been commissioned by him to effect the destruction of the idol temples of Amber, the ancient capital of Jaipur, reported in person that three score and six of these edifices had been levelled with the ground.'

It was Aurangzeb who put Guru Teg Bahadur, the ninth Guru of the Sikhs, to death in Dihli. According to the author of the Dabistan the emperor ordered the Guru's body to be quartered and the parts thereof to be suspended at the four gates of the city. Aurangzeb also persecuted Guru Gobind

Singh, the tenth and last Guru of the Sikhs, and forced him to fly from the Panjab; and it was a result of the same monarch's tyranny that Guru Gobind Singh's four sons lost their lives and that none of his descendants survived.

Many sincere thinkers and reformers lived under the above and other Zizlamic emperors of Zindia, but they were either executed or if they lived they were not allowed to write of the atrocities or record much of their teachings.

Sadly that tyrant barbarian Aurangzeb remains well honored in Zindia with a well maintained monument of his grave where Zizlamists zealously make pilgrimages, and with important city and road named after him.

ADHARMA

Vidyā-putra Veni-prasād, a wandering sadhu from a kali-yuga of two billion years ago, is on a pilgrimage and has stopped at a village to rest. Here he is talking to people sitting under a banyan tree. Vidyā-putra said: "

Just as we see in the Bhagavad-Gītā, in this world we always find two forces lined up in confrontation. This is a conflict most ancient, a battle that seemingly rages endlessly—and it is the war which Adharma is always waging against Dharma. Wherever there is Dharma Adharma too will be found standing in opposition—in fact as a force that's a hundred times larger. Why so? Because Dharma requires the hard work of penance, restrain, self-control, while Adharma is it very opposite: ease and sleaze; fully giving in to urges of pleasures and desires; enjoy now and who the hell cares of future—of which ideology there are so many customers.

No wonder of Dharma there are hardly any takers and Adharma sells so well, especially because they have perfected the art of displaying just the bright glittering side of life—with the seamy, dark, and sad swept into the dustbin—where most of the perpetrators end up eventually; because while you may end up cheating the world, but there is no cheating the reality and inevitability of karma, separation, disease, decay, death.

For example you will find Adharma showcasing these long lines of successful, sexy, young revellers merrily marching in a festive parade—with the camera focus always held upon that one spot of the moving belt: where the young, beautiful, successful, rich are clustered together; and while the faces and bodies keep changing, but the gay parade keeps riveted just on the spot where they are seen entering the glittering arena, sprouting like beautiful flowers in bloom, with people rising on their feet and cheering and applauding them to high heavens; and although they are continually being replaced on that moving line by an ever new crop of humans emerging daily on earth, the camera never shifts to show what really becomes of them later on—when they get old and lose their fortunes and become beset with disease, decay, death—the inevitabilities of life. Nay, let's just be showcasing just the goody goody stuff that sells well and let's keep sweeping the realities of life under the rug.

The idea is just to sell false dreams built on surrendering wholeheartedly to the abundance of sense-pleasures, whereas showing the other side—pain, disease, death, decay, breakups, loneliness sorrow—would simply spoil the fun and their sham dreams won't sell anymore. The intent and message is clear: enjoy, enjoy, enjoy; join the fun parade of external pleasures because that's all there's to life: succumb fully to the sense cravings that are being bedecked and paraded before you; just have fun—the realities of life be damned.

Fact is that this world is an abode of sorrows and there is absolutely no happiness in this glittering world of sense-pleasures. Beautiful materialistic hollow dreams are being sold by the world-ruling elites, and also false hopes and promises by the sham religious-sects—pretensions being peddled on the world stage on a massive scale, each having their own method of implementing their chicanery but with one common agenda—feeding off of people's life, money, soul; and rape the earth, and barren it of her beauty and her beautiful creatures. And sadly no one is protesting or doing anything about it—or if the do, most are simply crushed, having no resources to fight back.

Today Adharma dominates the entire world in the shape of a system which is really a work of genius—fully matured and perfected to a T—by the handful of ruling-elites and of course the two fraud religions under their patronage, who together hold the entire world by their, well—reproductive glands that produce spermatozoa and secrete androgens—selling them materialistic dreams and tales of rapacity and fun-galore—just so they can get to dig even deeper into people's pockets, make money off of them, get to rule over their lives and souls.

It was a Herculean effort and took centuries to perfect, but they have managed it quite well and now they are here to stay, ruling over us like the Lords they are—until of course the day of reckoning when the whole world they have created, and which we the people have allowed without a whimper in protest, collapses like a packs of cards. Had people learnt of the Ekam-Sanātana-Dharma and woken up to the danger and challenged it much earlier on, the cost in terms of lives of humans and other creatures wouldn't be so enormous as it will be now.

Ekam-Sanātana-Dharma tells the human of his reality—who man truly is; freeing him from external bondages, from the slavery to sense-objects; telling him that real success means gaining freedom and becoming supreme—above all gaining mastery over his own mind; giving man the means to acquire control over himself, completely freeing him from all bondages until one day that man can arise and proclaim: verily I am God, eternally perfect, eternally free, eternally in bliss, eternally abiding—never any death for me.

By contrast Adharma goes to great lengths to hide the reality of man; keeping him in bounds to the world of senses; promoting promiscuity, enslaving him to sense pleasures; telling the man that happiness is only in worldly things—that blessedness comes only from amassing money and gaining power over others—which alone defines success, always seeking validations from others, always aspiring to be the man on stage whom the world is applauding, becoming famous, turning into an over-achiever, always in race to get ahead of others by all means fair and foul—or else you are just an effing loser not worth living; telling man that happiness consists of accumulate things—all of which the dream-seller elites themselves are producing and selling.

And the charade continues with their Thatrī-barā Adhārmika sects telling man that he was born in sin and so must ever remain guilty, or be remaining bowed before a fomo who ostensibly paid for all the sins of all of humanity for all times to come—so long as you just be sucking up to him, his books, his zhurch, his clerics—aye, that's all it takes, just saying "aye" to the man the magical savior; and of course to lighten one's guilt one should keep lightening one's pockets, forking over his money to the middle-men to feel better; or with them telling man to gain a great sense of self worth not by self-effort but by dint of their perceived self-superiority and hatred of others—because those are not of his faith and are therefore inferior, and so they should be pitied, hated, converted, killed—take your pick; and of course nailing it into the head of the foolish flock that their greatest duty is to kill the infidels and that will take you straight to heavens where their god has a factory producing a ready supply of virgins for them to nail night and day—for that is the greatest thing in life right?—be banging 72 hoors all the while, and drinking wine with rivers of milk, honey, booze flowing by.

Adharma conditions you into believing that if you are towing the line—dating and having fun-filled weekends, watching sports, visiting restaurants, operas, theatres, eating, drinking, consuming, cruising, vacationing—in general spending money on frivolous things to keep their system going—and devouring their goods like gluttons, injecting fat into arteries and then becoming sick to keep their pharmaceutical and doctors rich—then you are a regular good old Joe for whom—my god, my dog, my cuntry, my flag, my country, my kind, my color, my beer, my zezus, my book, my zhurch—is all there's to life and religion, and the rest all-just-be-damned; and if you are not towing their line, then you are just an effing loser not worth living.

Dharma frees; and Adharma raises humans like on chicken farms, feeding off of them—for the ruling-elites to drain off their blood— and for their pontiffz, mullaz, priestz to be gathering and fleecing the flock and harvesting their souls.

Dharma sees you as an individual; Adharma sees you as mass produced pavlovian-human that will react predictably to their jingles and continue making them rich.

Dharma has for its foundations the Vedas which have been existence for hundreds of thousands of years, which scriptures are the foundation of humanity, which humanity has managed to exist so far and for so long because some humans somewhere kept protecting the Vedas and Dharma and most all others could therefore abide under the grace of Dharma's protection. Mind it, all morality springs directly from Sanātana-Dharma—because she establishes that that 'other' yonder is none other than I myself.

Adharma has sham religion as its foundation based on books concocted few centuries ago; or it has for its foundation that which their mind tells them they do, impelled by need of the hour or the alluring sense-objects; and so they have as their basis dung-load of divergent theories of diverse traits, mostly at odds with each other, having no history of successes behind—and by success we mean that which has been proven over the span of millenniums; and although themselves in severe conflict against each other, they are united on one front: annihilate Sanātana-Dharma.

And why is Sanātana-Dharma marked out for this special treatment? Because Sanātana-Dharma is iconoclastic, is a system liberating of humans, a great philosophy brought forth on earth by an intelligent proud people who couldn't condone slavery; whereas Adharma is all about keeping people enslaved so that these meffing charlatans can continue to rule and profiteer off of people forced into living dark sad slavish existences.

Dharma recognize that we are a consciousness rooted in Braham and we have been doing the rounds of births and deaths in this world and we should get out of this cycle of sorrows and merge back in Braham, the ocean of bliss.

Adharma takes the opposite view saying that our consciousness is just some chemical reaction and this life just happened by accident and this living breathing body is all there is and upon death nothing happens, or some believe that we remain buried in grave till the bones rot and some miracle happens if we are obedient and toe the line and kiss up to of a special man called the prophet whom alone God favors!

Adharma assert that there is no God, no maker; and that life ensued as a result of chemical reaction—as to how the chemical itself works of that they have no clue; and when Sanātana-Dharma tells them that even behind that chemistry and physics is Braham and if they delve to the very depth of things, nothing will be found but the consciousness of Braham—then they just stand there in denial, with a blank look, for they don't have the mental capacity to comprehend any of that—being they have never bothered to delve into the study of their own consciousness. Or Adharma have these childish stories of a human like god sitting somewhere in heaven who has this agent, a special man called god's prophet—and which man everyone must follow or be converted or eliminated.

Dharma believes that there's one ocean of consciousness in existence called Braham; and that it is He that has become manifest as the universe; and that the universe is nothing but one homogenous whole bereft of duality; and that at the root of my "I" is the Ātmā which remain rooted in Braham; and my awareness emanates from that Ātmā—albeit it becomes sullied as it flows out; that at its nascency, my awareness is just pure bliss and consciousness; and that my sense of existence and time emanates from my Ātmā; and that the goal of my existence is to remove the stain of superimpositions which are tainting my pure awareness; and that having thus restored my nascent awareness I will abide in everlasting bliss, and there is never any death for me. I am immortal bliss and nothing else.

THE ZINDOOS OF ZINDIA

Vidyā-putra Veni-prasād, a wandering sadhu from a kali-yuga of two billion years ago, is on a pilgrimage and has stopped at a village to rest. Here he is talking to people sitting under a banyan tree. Vidyā-putra said: "

Braham is the One-God and sages call Him variously and there are several paths leading to that One-Supreme—that is what Sanātana-Dharma teaches us. In the Bhagavad-Gītā Lord Krishna says:

— ॐ —

ये यथा मां प्रपद्यन्ते तांस्तथैव भजाम्यहम् ।
ye yathā māṁ prapadyante tāṁstathaiva bhajāmyaham
मम वर्त्मानुवर्तन्ते मनुष्याः पार्थ सर्वशः ॥४-११॥
mama vartmānuvartante manuṣyāḥ pārtha sarvaśaḥ (BG-4-11)

By whatsoever means men worship Me, I reciprocate likewise and accept them on their terms. In all ways, O Pārtha, all beings tread on paths that eventually are seen leading just to Me.

When we realize the truth of Braham—that all this is one existence and there's nothing else here but Braham—our vision becomes broad and all-encompassing, all-embracing, and we remain understanding and respectful of others and of the fact there are many paths leading to the supreme with diverse people treading various paths to reach the goal. But that is where it should stop—with seeing and accepting the universality but not necessarily be embracing each and everything—including the vile, evil, despicable, ugly, nauseous—and holding everything and everyone close to our hearts.

Nay, that is so very wrong; and it is exactly that wrongness which the Zindoos have come to embrace these past several centuries—this faulty idea of universally embracing all, even the openly inimical and your sworn destroyers—this notion of toleration of even the repulsive, repugnant, evil and that which is decreed as Adharma by Sanātana-Dharma—simply out of stupidity and cowardice cloaked under the guise of brotherly all-is-Braham love, which teaching Sanātana-Dharma never dispenses.

It is just the cowards, manipulators and fake-guruz who have been teaching this BS to Zindoos in the name of Zindooism, but which teaching is nowhere found in the Vedas or our histories recorded in the Ramayana and Mahabharata. Do not accept verses plucked out of context and thrown at you to spread a nefarious agenda, but better study your scriptures in original to fully understand of Ekam-Sanātana-Dharma.

Zindoos have becomes too broad-minded and large-hearted for their own good, and they have continued with their embrace of a sickening infantile ideal of tolerance, tightening that hug even further in recent times—which in fact is a thin cloak draped upon their arrant cravenness and imbecility.

Zindoos keep patting themselves on the back proudly asserting there never has been any persecution in Zindia of people of other faiths and that is true; but Sanātana-Dharma never teaches that Adharma should be tolerated. On the contrary you will discover upon reading the Mahabharata and Ramayana, that Sanātana-Dharma exhorts that Adharma be resisted with all one's might and mercilessly rooted out.

Though all is Braham—and when we do get to that realization we can clearly discern that indeed everyone and everything is Braham—but then upon reaching that realization either the body drops off—its Prarabdha exhausted and the Ātmā merges in Braham; or else the mind congeals and we return to reality and continue living in the world in this body to work out our remnant Prarabdha, i.e., continue living until it's finally our time to depart from the world—as decreed by our karma-driven destiny. And while we live in the body, we do what the human body does—put food into the mouth when hungry and drink water when thirsty. We do not put excreta and sewage in the mouth thinking all is same from the Vedantic viewpoint and so anything goes, all are equal, let me eat anything, partake of anything; and let me embrace my neighbor's wife as if my own; and let me embrace even the guy who has the knife on my mother's throat. Yes all is same, but from the practical viewpoint of the collective, distinctions have to be clearly maintained—or else the structure of society itself will crumble and human existence cannot continue into the future.

Although all the paths on which people are wending their ways are found eventually leading just to Braham—with some paths easy; some short, straight but hard; some longish and charming, some passing through lovely landscapes, some roads paved with hell, some winding and tortuous, some that take just one life time to reach Braham, and some very convoluted with first having to undergo hell and torment experiencing nightmarish existences before turning back to reach Braham after millions of births—but that doesn't mean that we condone all those ways or embrace them ourselves—because some are too abhorrent and vile; such paths which first put you on a tour to the very depths of infernal agony—before turning upwards again; paths that put your journey back to Braham in deep regression—setting you back many a births.

And it is okay if certain individuals take the evil routes—and we can be tolerant of that and not even interfere in their life to show them what we perceive to be the "our-right-way"—for who the hell are we in judgment of that—unless they ask us for help; but it is certainly not okay if some madmen band together and start spreading their malevolent ways through aggression, crusades, holy-wars, zihads, calling everyone else a dirty unbeliever targeted to be killed or converted by all means fair and foul.

Aye, eventually one day we will all merge in Braham—but some will reach there sooner and with little pain—following the paths of Sanātana-Dharma; and others will reach there after a long dreadful journey spanning millions of births with enormous periods on that journey filled with hell, torture, pain—just as in the paths of the sham religious sects.

From Braham's perspective, He doesn't give a damn which path we humans take—because He spun out this creation merely as a sport and He has infinite time at hand and is no hurry and with little else to do; and if He finds people taking the long painful road to hell, it's all the more fun for Him. Aye, from Braham's perspective, it is all a sport, and the crazier the better, since Braham delights in macabre bizarre shows—like for instance Zizlamists massacring 100's of millions of helpless Zindoos who kept cowering and couldn't devise a strategy fast enough against blood curdling terror—but it's not okay from the perspective of humans that are living as families and society, with their everything at stake.

As humans yes, we do have to give a damn—unlike Braham who doesn't; and unto the Zindoos who still keep cowering and stupidly keep insisting on embracing their Zizistian and Zizlamic brethrens who have been converting and killing them for centuries, we have to kick their behinds to jar them awake from their daze. Currently the Zindoo guruz are like: its all Braham's sport so let us just be kneeling and get slaughtered some more—instead they have to wake up, rise, resist, fight back.

For those living as householders and have families to protect, they have wake up to the danger and devise best strategies to cope with the situation where the enemies of Sanātana-Dharma have openly declared their agenda of making Zindia an Zizlamic nation by 2047—meaning anyone who is not a Zizlamist must either convert or be killed, as happened in the East and West Zakistans where just a few centuries ago everyone was a Zindoo but no more now. But the Zindoo is blind to the history and graph of Zizlamic growth—on an upward geometrical progression like a rising crescent—and their only strategy is in just trying to embrace the Zizlamists and hold him close to their hearts saying—"Hey bro, see we love you, so why can't you?" The Zizlamist just keeps quiet and doesn't say to his face but is laughing inside saying—"Because my book says that it is my duty to eliminate all infidels from earth."

It is amazing how the Zizlamists does his fully-faulty-decreed-duty so well, whereas despite Krishna's repeated exhortations in the Gītā—"Do your darned duty dude"—the Zindoo keeps ignoring his God's teaching and remains worshipping Him just in temples. A more shameless foolish people than the hypocrite Zindoos do not exist on earth. They have not cared to learn from history, nor are they looking at the graph of how the Zizlamists are multiplying as if on a military-mission, nor have they read the history or the authentic books of these people whose faith tells them that everyone who's not of their faiths is a dirty being on earth—to be converted or purged.

When it comes to evil, Sanātana-Dharma teaches aloofness and attitude of empathy—but only so long as it is just an individual thing, but when that rot begins to spread and affect the integrity of society and corrupts and defiles people, then not only you do not tolerate it, but you fight back and punish it and eradicate that madness forever.

If five times a day a crazed man brays like a donkey sitting alongside his goat, rotating his neck facing the moon, and then violates the modesty of that goat at midnight, and on the fortieth day he slaughters it painfully and slowly and eats it—and further insists on calling all that as his religion, then so be it; and you can choose to be broadminded and simply ignore it so long as he does it in the privacy of his home; but if he goes around insisting that other too should follow his 'religion' and moreover employs cunning and force to spread his madness, then you do not embrace him saying—O all religions are same—but instead banish such madness out of society.

To condone and embrace even madness in the name of all-is-Braham and all paths are paths to Braham, is not tolerance but validating insanity—and is a sinful thing to do, and this is what the Zindoos have been doing—validating the shams of Zizistianity and Zizlam to hide the fact that they are just too cowardly to resist them. All the plethora of fake-zindoo-guruz can be seen sucking up to these shams sects, without as much as studying their books, and they sit on stages and go about bandying worn out fictive phrases like Sarva-Dharma-Sambhāva —all religions are equal.

99 the Zindoos of Zindia

Zindoo is the only fool who insists that all religions are equal, whereas the follower of every religion on earth says that my religion is the best. And just for that foolishness Braham has allowed them to be slaughtered by the 100's of millions over the centuries and did not as much as shed a tear let alone provide any help. Nature doesn't aid cowards and dullards—only the strong and the fit survive per nature's law. And this carnage will continue—it is clear as daylight—and Braham wouldn't do a thing to help out these cowering pudden-heads, because you see in Braham's nature only the strong, intelligent are meant to survive and not the asleep, dazed, demented, dullard, laggards.

If Nature starts rewarding mild sheepish cowering flock, the meek of the earth, just because they have wrongly assumed that God is on their side, then creation will screech to a halt within a millennium, and Braham will have to call off the whole thing as a flop, cancel the whole darn show. Of course He would never allow it, you can bet on that. So Zindoos you better wake up to the realities of life and stop worshipping Krishna just only as an idol in temples but listen to what He said in the Bhagavad-Gītā. Listen and act on Krishna's words—that alone is the real worship of Lord-God Krishna.

In the Bhagavad-Gītā Krishna says that He is the incarnate form of Braham, and all creation and all these being are from Him, and it is He who abides dwelling within the hearts of all:

—ॐ—

अहं कृत्स्नस्य जगतः प्रभवः प्रलयस्तथा ॥७-६॥

ahaṁ kṛtsnasya jagataḥ prabhavaḥ pralayastathā (BG-7-6)

[Lord-God Krishna says:] I am the origin of this entire creation, and into Me again everything submerges in the end.

—ॐ—

अधियज्ञोऽहमेवात्र देहे देहभृतां वर ॥८-४॥

adhiyajño'hamevātra dehe dehabhṛtāṁ vara (8-4)

It is I myself, as the *Adhiyajna,* who dwells as the inner witness in all embodied beings.

And yet the same Lord-God Krishna tells Arjuna a couple chapter later in the same book—i.e., a few minutes later on the battlefield—to fight and put down Adharma for good.

— ॐ —

द्रोणं च भीष्मं च जयद्रथं च कर्णं तथान्यानपि योधवीरान् ।
droṇaṁ ca bhīṣmaṁ ca jayadrathaṁ ca karṇaṁ tathānyānapi yodhavīrān
मया हतांस्त्वं जहि मा व्यथिष्ठा युध्यस्व जेतासि रणे सपत्नान् ॥ ११-३४ ॥
mayā hatāṁstvaṁ jahi mā vyathiṣṭhā yudhyasva jetāsi raṇe sapatnān (11-34)

Fight and kill Drona and Bhīshma and Jayadratha and Karna, and all these other mighty warriors—all slayed by Me already. Fear not; fight on, and you shall surely conquer your enemies in this battle.

Drona and Bhīshma are the gurus and elders of Arjuna whom Arjuna has held in embrace for too long, but now they are on the side of Adharma and so Krishna tells Arjuna to fight them and others on Adharma's side unto death; for Adharma cannot be allowed to become the prevalent mode in society or else society comes to ruin. Only the goodness of Dharma should remain as the predominant force in the world for a healthy society to subsist.

Do not make the mistake of learning Sanātana-Dharma from just few verses thrown at you plucked from here and there, but instead make an in-depth study of it by carefully studying its ancient scriptures like the Upanishads, Ramayana, Bhagavad-Gītā etc., in original. Beware of people who have their own axes to grind, or are propagating their own sects, or are Kālnemis—people actually from the opposition but posing as Zindoos.

— ॐ —

Sītā-Rāma-Hanumān is my Lord-God; I surrender my life to Him; I placed Sītā-Rāma in my heart and wrote as the inspiration flowed; but I am an extremely broken instrument for this task—with defective learning, an imperfect understanding of Sanātana-Dharma, and poor language and style—and consequently this book is full of faults. Please ignore whatever I have written—after all this is just a work of fiction—and discover Sanātana-Dharma directly for yourself, by making an in-depth study of the Bhagavad-Gītā and other Upanishads, and the Rāmāyana and Mahābhārata, always staying focused on the original while remaining skeptic of extensive commentaries and interpretations. *

—— जय हनुमान -: ॐ :- जय सीताराम ——

* Thank you for reading thus far. If you liked this, we have a few more books lined up; please check them out later. **Jai Hanumān, Jai Shri Sītā-Rāma.**

sundar-kānda

the fifth-ascent of

rāmacharita-mānas

— जय श्रीसीताराम —

— श्रीजानकीवल्लभो विजयते —

—: श्रीरामचरितमानस :—

पञ्चम सोपान – सुन्दरकाण्ड

श्लोक

शान्तं शाश्वतमप्रमेयमनघं निर्वाणशान्तिप्रदं
ब्रह्माशम्भुफणीन्द्रसेव्यमनिशं वेदान्तवेद्यं विभुम् ।
रामाख्यं जगदीश्वरं सुरगुरुं मायामनुष्यं हरिं
वन्देऽहं करुणाकरं रघुवरं भूपालचूडामणिम् ॥ १ ॥

नान्या स्पृहा रघुपते हृदयेऽस्मदीये
सत्यं वदामि च भवानखिलान्तरात्मा ।
भक्तिं प्रयच्छ रघुपुङ्गव निर्भरां मे
कामादिदोषरहितं कुरु मानसं च ॥ २ ॥

अतुलितबलधामं हेमशैलाभदेहं
दनुजवनकृशानुं ज्ञानिनामग्रगण्यम् ।
सकलगुणनिधानं वानराणामधीशं
रघुपतिप्रियभक्तं वातजातं नमामि ॥ ३ ॥

चौपाई

जामवंत के बचन सुहाए । सुनि हनुमंत हृदय अति भाए ॥
तब लगि मोहि परिखेहु तुम्ह भाई । सहि दुख कंद मूल फल खाई ॥
जब लगि आवौं सीतहि देखी । होइहि काजु मोहि हरष बिसेषी ॥
यह कहि नाइ सबन्हि कहुँ माथा । चलेउ हरषि हियँ धरि रघुनाथा ॥
सिंधु तीर एक भूधर सुंदर । कौतुक कूदि चढ़ेउ ता ऊपर ॥
बार बार रघुबीर सँभारी । तरकेउ पवनतनय बल भारी ॥
जेहिं गिरि चरन देइ हनुमंता । चलेउ सो गा पाताल तुरंता ॥

[...]

चौपाई

नाथ नील नल कपि द्वौ भाई । लरिकाईं रिषि आसिष पाई ॥
तिन्ह कें परस किएँ गिरि भारे । तरिहहिं जलधि प्रताप तुम्हारे ॥
मैं पुनि उर धरि प्रभु प्रभुताई । करिहउँ बल अनुमान सहाई ॥
एहि बिधि नाथ पयोधि बँधाइअ । जेहिं यह सुजसु लोक तिहुँ गाइअ ॥
एहिं सर मम उत्तर तट बासी । हतहु नाथ खल नर अघ रासी ॥
सुनि कृपाल सागर मन पीरा । तुरतहिं हरी राम रनधीरा ॥
देखि राम बल पौरुष भारी । हरषि पयोनिधि भयउ सुखारी ॥
सकल चरित कहि प्रभुहि सुनावा । चरन बंदि पाथोधि सिधावा ॥

छंद

निज भवन गवनेउ सिंधु श्रीरघुपतिहि यह मत भायऊ ।
यह चरित कलि मलहर जथामति दास तुलसी गायऊ ॥
सुख भवन संसय समन दवन बिषाद रघुपति गुन गना ।
तजि सकल आस भरोस गावहि सुनहि संतत सठ मना ॥

दोहा

सकल सुमंगल दायक रघुनायक गुन गान ।
सादर सुनहिं ते तरहिं भव सिंधु बिना जलजान ॥ ६० ॥

इति श्रीमद्रामचरितमानसे सकलकलिकलुषविध्वंसने
पञ्चमः सोपानः समाप्तः

śrī hanumāna cālīsā

श्री हनुमान चालीसा

[illegible]

aṣṭāvakra-gītā

॥ श्रीमदष्टावक्र गीता ॥

:: Canto – I ::
- Instructions on Self-Realization -

जनक उवाच
janaka uvāca:
कथं ज्ञानमवाप्नोति कथं मुक्तिर्भविष्यति ।
वैराग्यं च कथं प्राप्तमेतद् ब्रूहि मम प्रभो ॥ १-१ ॥
अष्टावक्र उवाच
aṣṭāvakra uvāca:
मुक्तिमिच्छसि चेत्तात विषयान् विषवत्त्यज ।
क्षमार्जवदयातोषसत्यं पीयूषवद् भज ॥ १-२ ॥
न पृथ्वी न जलं नाग्निर्न वायुर्द्यौर्न वा भवान् ।
एषां साक्षिणमात्मानं चिद्रूपं विद्धि मुक्तये ॥ १-३ ॥
यदि देहं पृथक् कृत्य चिति विश्राम्य तिष्ठसि ।
अधुनैव सुखी शान्तो बन्धमुक्तो भविष्यसि ॥ १-४ ॥
न त्वं विप्रादिको वर्णो नाश्रमी नाक्षगोचरः ।
असङ्गोऽसि निराकारो विश्वसाक्षी सुखी भव ॥ १-५ ॥
धर्माधर्मौ सुखं दुःखं मानसानि न ते विभो ।
न कर्तासि न भोक्तासि मुक्त एवासि सर्वदा ॥ १-६ ॥
एको द्रष्टासि सर्वस्य मुक्तप्रायोऽसि सर्वदा ।
अयमेव हि ते बन्धो द्रष्टारं पश्यसीतरम् ॥ १-७ ॥

[illegible]

:: End Canto – I ::

:: Canto – II ::
- Reveling as the Ātmā -

[illegible]

:: End Canto – II ::

:: Canto – III ::
- Veracity of Self-Realization -

[illegible]

:: End Canto – III ::

:: Canto – IV ::
- Glory of Self-Realization -

[illegible]

:: End Canto – IV ::

:: Canto – V ::
- Dissolution -

[illegible]

:: End Canto – V ::

:: Canto – VI ::
- Supreme Truth -

[illegible]

:: End Canto – VI ::

:: Canto – VII ::
- Describing Self-Realization -

[illegible]

:: End Canto – VII ::

:: Canto – VIII ::
- Bondage and Liberation -

[illegible]

:: End Canto – VIII ::

:: Canto – IX ::
- Aloofness -

[illegible]

:: End Canto – IX ::

:: Canto – X ::
- Equanimity -

[illegible]

:: End Canto – X ::

:: Canto – XI ::
- Wisdom -

[illegible]

:: End Canto – XI ::

:: Canto – XII ::
- Onlyness -

[illegible]

:: End Canto – XII ::

:: Canto – XIII ::
- Felicity -

[illegible]

:: End Canto – XIII ::

:: Canto – XIV ::
- Tranquility -

[illegible]

:: End Canto – XIV ::

:: Canto – XV ::
- Essence of Science of Self-Knowledge -

[illegible]

:: End Canto – XV ::

:: Canto – XVI ::
- Special Instruction -

[illegible]

:: End Canto – XVI ::

:: Canto – XVII ::
- The Self-Realized Sage -

[illegible]

:: End Canto – XVII ::

:: Canto – XVIII ::
- Serenity -

[illegible]

:: End Canto – XVIII ::

:: Canto – XIX ::
- Reposing as the Ātmā -

[illegible]

:: End Canto – XIX ::

:: Canto – XX ::
- Liberation-in-Life -

[illegible]

:: End Canto – XX ::

pātañjala yoga-sūtrāṇi

॥ पातञ्जलयोगसूत्राणि ॥

॥ महर्षि पतञ्जलि प्रणीतं योगदर्शनम् ॥

॥ प्रथमोऽध्यायः समाधि-पादः ॥

[illegible]

॥ द्वितीयोऽध्यायः साधन-पादः ॥

[illegible]

॥ तृतीयोऽध्यायः विभूति-पादः ॥

[illegible]

॥ चतुर्थोऽध्यायः कैवल्य-पादः ॥

[illegible]

॥ इति श्री पातञ्जल-योग-सूत्राणि ॥

www.ingramcontent.com/pod-product-compliance
Lightning Source LLC
Chambersburg PA
CBHW080500240426
43673CB00006B/247

* 9 7 8 1 9 4 5 7 3 9 7 1 2 *